THE VICTIM
(and other short plays)

THE VICTIM
(and other short plays)

J. BOYETT

SALTIMBANQUE BOOKS

NEW YORK

BY THE SAME AUTHOR

Brothel
Ricky
Poisoned (a play)

DEDICATION:

To Mary Sheridan.

Also to Pam Carter, Dawn Drinkwater, and Andy Shanks.

Also to Tiffany Esteb, Kelly Kay Griffith, William Kozy, Kathryn McConnell, Bob Ost, Kenneth Ruth, and Brandi Varnell.

Also to my parents.

To others, as well.

THE VICTIM
(and other short plays)

TABLE OF
CONTENTS:

PART I

THE VICTIM

CHARACTERS:

APRIL: late twenties or early thirties.
GRACE: late twenties or early thirties.

SETTING:

April's apartment.

The play takes place in April's apartment. It can be performed with only a couple of chairs and a doorway, or something creatively set up to look like a doorway.
For the most part the actresses can move around however they like, except of course that Grace must be sitting in time for the stage direction "Grace rises."
Enter April and Grace, as if coming into the living room from a hallway; April's been giving Grace the tour. Both of them are uncomfortable; April seems embarrassed, Grace more sort of uncertain and out of her element.

APRIL

Well. That's the grand tour. My apartment. Voila.

GRACE

It's nice.

APRIL

Sorry it's such a mess. I should have cleaned more before you got here.

GRACE

I tried calling to let you know I was almost here, but. . . .

APRIL

Oh, yeah. Well, I realized about an hour ago that my phone's been shut off.

GRACE

Well . . . well, come here, give me a hug again! I'm so happy to see you!

APRIL

Yeah, me too.

They embrace.

GRACE

Wow, seeing you again. I have to say, when the whole Facebook fad started I thought, you will never catch me wasting time with that. But then . . . to be honest, I set up a profile mainly because I thought it would be a way to get back in touch with you.

APRIL

No way.

GRACE

Way.

APRIL

That's, that's why I set mine up, too. Was in the hopes of getting in touch with you.

GRACE

Really?

APRIL

Yeah, I . . . I'm sorry that I only ever sent you those short little bullshit replies, to your long chatty messages. I know it was probably rude. But I just. . . . I only wanted to talk about stuff in person. I'm not good at writing letters. I mean, maybe it would've been different if it hadn't turned out you were coming home in a month anyway, but. . . .

4

GRACE

Don't worry about it. . . . The other person I was going to look up was Steven. I didn't see him on your friends list. . . .

APRIL

Oh. No, I haven't been in touch with him for years.

GRACE

Mm. . . . Well, let's get caught up! I mean, God; how've you been?

APRIL

Oh, lately I've been kind of tired all the time . . . Jesus, I can't believe I said that, what a whiney thing to say. . . .

GRACE

Why tired?

APRIL

Oh, fucking work.

GRACE

Ah. Where are you working?

APRIL

Fucking Wal-Mart.

GRACE

Oh, yeah?

APRIL

Oh, yeah, real impressive. Biggest Supercenter in a town of Supercenters. Anyway, thanks for coming over.

GRACE

Well, of course. It's been too long. I kind of fell off the edge of the world—as far as everyone around here was concerned, anyway—but now I've resolved to climb back on.

APRIL

That's good. I kind of, I missed you.

5

GRACE

Oh, sweetie. I missed you, too. You and Steven are the only people in this town I've really missed, even including my own family.

APRIL

Wow, sounds like an honor. So, what, he's the one that got away?

GRACE

Well, no, that would be me. So . . . you don't happen to know where he is, do you?

APRIL

Steven?

GRACE

Yes.

APRIL

Well, he moved. About two years ago. Out of state.

GRACE

Oh. . . . Oh.

APRIL

Didn't you google him?

GRACE

I couldn't remember his last name.

APRIL

What? Steven's?

GRACE

About a month ago I realized how badly I wanted to see him again. And by then I couldn't remember his name anymore.

APRIL

Jesus, Grace. His name is Taylor.

GRACE

Taylor! Oh my God, that's right. Taylor.

APRIL

He moved to California. He married someone out there.

GRACE

Oh. . . . Well, anyway . . . wow! I don't even know what to say! It's so crazy to be seeing you again! It's been years and years, and we used to be so close. So . . . tell me all about what you've been up to for—man—the past however many years.

APRIL

It seems like you're the only one who's been up to stuff. All that traveling around and then that bigshot job in New York.

GRACE

No, well. I've done all right. But you must have been busy, too. I mean, it's been years. Obviously you must have been up to something.

APRIL

Well, you remember what happened nine years ago, right? The reason we stopped seeing each other around much?

GRACE

Uh. Refresh me.

APRIL

I dropped out of college. Freshman year.

GRACE

Oh. Yeah, that's right.

APRIL

Yeah. It is. Well, anyway, that's the last thing that happened that matters.

GRACE

Oh, come on. Don't say that, April.

APRIL

It's true.

GRACE

You're being dramatic. You left college and started working at the Wal-Mart Supercenter and haven't left since? You haven't dated anyone? Gone anywhere? In all those years?

APRIL
(impatiently)
Well, I dropped out and then started working at that Exxon on Woodlawn Boulevard. Then I worked at McDonald's. Then I had a whole series of shitty little jobs at places that may as well have been the same place, and the latest one of those is Wal-Mart. So, stuff's happened, but nothing's happened. I've dated a few guys, but it's sort of the same story as with the jobs, except that most of the guys were even shittier than the jobs. So I guess stuff has happened in that department, but I wish it hadn't. As far as going anyplace, I've only been out of the state maybe three times in all those years.

GRACE
Oh. *(Pause.)* April . . . is something wrong? Have I offended you? I mean, you asked me to come over. . . .

APRIL
It's just weirder than I thought it would be to see you again and have you be so successful. Even though I guess I always expected you to be successful.

GRACE
If you're upset because I let so much time slide by without contacting you, really it was nothing personal. I did the same thing with my own parents. Yesterday, when I got into town and went to my parents' house, that was the first time I'd seen anyone in my family in the last three years.

APRIL
I'm not mad. I'm nervous. About something to do with you.

GRACE
Oh. . . . I get it. Look. That job, these clothes, the salary, I just lucked into it. Really, April. Right place, right time, that's all. If I've come across as snooty, then I apologize. I hope you don't

think that I would ever look down on you because you work at
Wal-Mart.

APRIL
That's not what I'm nervous about.

GRACE
Well, then. . . . April, I know it's been a long time, but I'd like
everything between us to be. . . . What is it you're nervous
about?

APRIL
I'm going to ask you for something, is why.

GRACE
Then just ask.

APRIL
Shit. Shit, this is tough.

GRACE
April. Whatever it is, you don't have to get worked up.

APRIL
Okay. You remember how we basically stopped hanging out,
of course.

GRACE
Yeah. Freshman year, when you dropped out.

APRIL
What? No! No, before that. *You* remember. When we were
fifteen.

GRACE
Oh . . . but I saw you a lot after we were fifteen, didn't I?

APRIL
We saw each other, yeah; it's a small city, we went to the same
high school and the same college. For a while. But it wasn't like

before. We were best friends before that thing happened, when we were fifteen.

GRACE

Well. It's true, we did drift apart. But I don't remember some specific "thing" happening.

APRIL

You're not fucking serious.

GRACE

I'm sorry, April. But I mean, things were so crazy back then. We were so wild. Tell me which time you're talking about.

APRIL

My God. You've blocked it. I never realized people actually did that in real life.

GRACE

I don't think I've blocked anything. Although I guess the catch is that if I had then I wouldn't know.

APRIL

Grace. If you're fucking with me, then . . . please stop. I need you on this.

GRACE

Well, tell me what it is, April.

APRIL

I need someone's support and you're the only one who can give it. I can't do this on my own, Grace.

GRACE

Tell me what you need and I'll tell you if I can give it.

APRIL

You know what I'm talking about. You remember that party we went to? In the tenth grade?

GRACE
(laughing)
I'm afraid you'll have to be more specific.

APRIL

The one with all those older boys.

GRACE
(laughing harder)
Yeah, right. That's no help at all.

APRIL

All right, god damn it. *Peter.* That fucking college guy whose parents had that big, like, fucking mansion on Greenwood Avenue. His parents went out of town for the weekend and he invited all his frat brothers over for a big blow-out and you, too. And he told you to bring some friends, but you just brought me.

GRACE

Oh, God. I do remember that. Oh my God, what were we thinking? We were absolutely insane.

APRIL

I've always wondered why you invited me. Only me.

GRACE

Well, we were best friends, weren't we? More or less. We were always together those days, seems like.

APRIL

I guess maybe it was only that I couldn't help tagging along.

GRACE

Oh, wow. What were we thinking? My God, we were so wild and crazy and dumb.

APRIL

What, are you saying it was our fault?

GRACE

Our "fault"? . . . Well . . . yeah; I guess so.
Pause.

APRIL

I can't believe I'm hearing this. I can't believe it. From you.

11

Of all the people to hear something like that from, for it to be you. . . .

GRACE

But . . . well . . . who else's fault? I mean, our parents', I guess you could argue, but I don't want to. I guess it was shitty of the guys, them being so much older than us, but, well, they're guys, what do you expect. So, yeah, I guess it was our fault, but we were too young to know better, so I guess it was nobody's fault. And anyway all that was practically a lifetime ago. . . . Are you just talking about Peter's party in particular, or our whole, um, lifestyle back then?

APRIL

Fuck you.

GRACE

I beg your pardon?

APRIL

Fuck you. Fuck off. You're fucking with me. I have no clue why you'd do such a thing, but you are.

GRACE

I am? . . . Huh. You know, I come over to your house, we talk for five minutes, and you say something like that to me, something like "fuck you" . . . there was a time, and it's still so recent I have trouble remembering it's not still now, but there was a time when that would have been it. Understand? You would have said that, and I would have got up and walked out and never thought twice about it.

APRIL

So fucking do it. There's no one forcing you. *I'm* not forcing *you*.

GRACE

I won't do it because I decided a couple months ago to become a person who doesn't do stuff like that, who doesn't walk out.

APRIL

I haven't got a fucking clue what you're talking about.

GRACE

Well I wish you'd go about trying to figure it out some other way.

APRIL

You tell me about the party.

GRACE

The party at Peter's?

APRIL

The party at Peter's.

GRACE

Um; sure, I'll try. It's been over a decade, you know.

APRIL

Jesus. All right, fine. Just try.

GRACE

All right. . . . Well. You and I went alone. Obviously that was dumb, since who knows what we would have done if things had gotten . . . you know . . . but that was the kind of stupid thing we used to do all the time back then, wasn't it? Peter's parents had a big pool in the back yard, and everybody stripped to their underwear and you and I hopped into the pool along with all those frat boys. I remember, the pool had really bright underwater lights, so that it glowed like an electric sapphire in the black back yard. . . . I remember thinking of this line a few years ago, about how a pool with its underwater lamps on at night is like a jewel and the night is the velvet it's set against, and then I wrote a whole poem just so I could use the line. Maybe it was actually Peter's pool I was thinking of, subconsciously. Oh, but, hey, I digress. . . . Anyway, while we were horsing around with all those guys, someone switched off the pool lights. . . . Jesus, April, are you crying?

APRIL

No, keep going. I need to hear you say it, I need to hear it. Please.

GRACE

Well . . . well, once those pool lights were out, you and I started making out with all those boys. All those boys, in the dark—we couldn't really see them, we just swam from one to the other, kissing them, our bodies covered in hands. One time we swam into each other on accident—or else the boys maneuvered us into each other—we giggled, and kissed a little, to get the boys hot, and they were all hooting and hollering.

APRIL

And then.

GRACE

Well, it didn't take long after that before we all went back inside and had sex in the living room. You and I were in different parts of the room. Everyone was drunk and stoned by then, but even so I guess that between the two of us we laid every guy there. And then . . . we didn't spend the night there, I'm sure . . . but where did we go? We couldn't possibly have gone to either of our parents' houses, not reeking of weed and alcohol like that . . . so where did we tell our parents we were spending the night? . . . No, I can't remember. Do you remember?
Pause.

APRIL

Yes. I remember. *(Pause.)* You. I mean. What? Like, what the fuck?

GRACE

April?

APRIL

I mean, what are you telling me?

GRACE

I just told you.

APRIL

No, I mean . . . can't you say it?

14

GRACE

April, it's pretty much as clear as could be that you and I are on different wavelengths here, so maybe you should just come out and say . . . whatever it is.

APRIL

I was so jealous. I was so jealous of you, because you'd gotten out, and you were doing great. I was so pissed at you for being stronger than I was. And proud of you, too. But I was wrong, wasn't I?

GRACE

I . . . well, I don't know of any reason to think I'm stronger than you, so, yeah, I suppose that possibly you were wrong.

APRIL

Oh, honey. I thought you were going to come over here and rescue me. Be all no-bullshit like I remembered you being. But I didn't realize. Oh, you're more fucked-up than I am.

GRACE

Okay.

APRIL

This is a story you've told yourself. You were so ashamed of what had happened that you had to figure out some way out of it, so you made up this story. And now you've been rehearsing it to yourself so long that it's turned into second nature, you really believe it.

GRACE

April, I haven't "rehearsed" anything. This is the first time I've even thought of that party in quite a while. I was doing stuff like that from the ages of twelve to seventeen. And you know that.

APRIL

But on some level you know what really happened, and you're not doing yourself any favors by burying it. Those boys took us back into the house and raped us.

15

GRACE

What?

APRIL

But we're going to get them now. Don't worry. You and me, we're going to get our, you know, our lives back. We're going to press charges. You just have to say it.

GRACE

What?

APRIL

Don't be scared.

GRACE

April. April, nobody's raped *me*. And nobody raped you, either—at least not that night.

APRIL

Listen. Hey—don't you or anybody else fucking tell me what happened that night, okay. Okay? I'm fucking, from now on *I'm* fucking telling people what happened to me that night.

GRACE

April. You've got to be responsible, there's other people involved. . . . Are you sure you mean *Peter's* house? Are we definitely talking about the same night? Maybe you're conflating it with something else—

APRIL

Fuck you! Fuck you!

GRACE

All right, okay, just calm down, I didn't mean—

APRIL

I'm not inflating anything! I'm just saying what happened! I'm not exaggerating one fucking thing!

GRACE

Not "inflating." "Conflating." But listen, it doesn't matter. . . .

APRIL

"Conflating"? What the hell is that?

GRACE

It means, like, mixing up or combining two separate things. Like maybe there were similar circumstances at a different party, where you *were* raped, and now you've put the two parties together so that you think this thing actually happened at Peter's party, the one you and I were at together. . . .

APRIL

Oh. Oh, fuck you. If you fucking one more time tell me what I. . . . Anyway, why couldn't you just say that, huh? What, is that one of your college words? Your fucking "conflating"?

Pause.

GRACE

I guess maybe it is. I wasn't trying to come across as anything.

APRIL

We were raped.

GRACE

I don't remember being raped.

APRIL

Listen, I'm sorry I flew off the handle. It's just, it's taken me so long to get to a point where I can talk about it. Because . . . it would have been different, you know. If I'd been walking along a dark street and some guy in a ski mask had jumped out and pulled me into an alley and hit me and forced me. Then I would have been able to tell people. But as it was, it took me a while to figure things out. To even realize what had happened. And by the time I'd decided, it felt too late to tell people. And anyway . . . like, how could I have told my parents? How could I have even explained going to that fucking party? They would have crucified me. I would've been, what, grounded, and that would have been the end of it. Maybe they would have called Peter's parents to complain. Whatever. I remember, I felt so stupid

17

and dirty and ugly after those assholes were done. And it hurt, I was really sore. And I figured it was all my fault, for not doing like my family said and for acting like a whore. I was a kid and so I thought it was all my fault. But now I look back. Now I look back and because I'm a grown-up looking back at a kid I see that it wasn't my fault. I see whose fault it was.

Pause.

GRACE
Peter's.

APRIL
Yes. You see.

GRACE
I meant it more like a question.

APRIL
What is there to question? God damn it!

GRACE
Okay. Just tell me exactly what it is you're asking me for, April.

APRIL
I *need* you.

GRACE
What is it you need?

APRIL
For one thing I need you to testify with me. I need you to press charges with me.

GRACE
Oh.

APRIL
Otherwise . . . how will I have a chance? We have a chance? Some nobody, some loser, some dumb bitch college dropout who works at Wal-Mart, who started fucking people when she

was thirteen—who'll believe me? That's why I need you, too. Together they won't be able to ignore us.

GRACE

Who won't be able?

APRIL

The courts, the lawyers, the cops, I don't know. All of them, those guys.

GRACE

I don't see how I can exactly bolster your credibility. I started having sex when I was twelve, you know.

APRIL

I know, but see, you're so different now. Look at you, you're a success, anybody can see that. Just by your face. Me, the jury will think I'm bitter about all sorts of other shit. But you, they'll listen to.

GRACE

I'm not sure being a successful career woman—i. e. uppity bitch—has always been an advantage in the witness box.

APRIL

You're tough. I need you.

GRACE

April. I'm not sure I can help you. Because I don't feel raped.

APRIL

Oh, for—okay, just talk to me. Just talk to me a little while.

GRACE

I'll talk to you for as long as you want.

APRIL

Okay. Okay. So tell me. How did you feel? After it happened?

Pause.

19

GRACE

I felt awful, partly. I felt stupid and kind of dirty. And I remembered that I'd felt like that when I was twelve, too—when I was first really having sex with boys—but I'd made myself get out of the habit of feeling that way. I was a child so it made sense to think what I felt was childish, and I figured this was a stupid, kiddy way to feel, and I didn't want to be a kid. I wanted to be fearless and grown-up. To do grown-up things. I wanted to see how far I could go—I wanted to prove that I could go just as far as anyone else, as far as anyone anywhere could. I'd gotten used to having sex, and I thought I liked it; but this was my first time with the whole assembly-line thing, and it felt weird and embarrassing. But I wanted to prove that I could take on anybody, anything, any way, because nothing tied me down. So then, after it was all over, I felt ashamed of myself for feeling ashamed. If that makes any sense. . . . But don't get me wrong, I also felt charged. You know, that rush you get after you've torn yourself down, after you've been totally blasted through, and then you find yourself still going.

APRIL

Did you ask them to stop?

GRACE

Oh, well. . . .

APRIL

Did you fucking tell them to stop? I know you did. We both did.

GRACE

Yeah, but only at first, and only half-joking.

APRIL

Half-joking?!

GRACE

I changed my mind before we even got started. And I didn't even really mean it in the first place. I was coy and nervous.

20

APRIL

You changed your mind. Okay, now you listen to me. I remember. I fucking remember. We left the pool. Someone grabbed my arm—fucking *Peter* grabbed my arm. Right above the fucking elbow. I said "Hey, let me go." And he just sort of laughed, and said "Huh-uh." And then I tried to pull away, I mean I'm fucking *physically trying to get away from this fucking guy,* and he's all like just grinning and shaking his fucking head and, and fucking *jabbing* me through his underwear and mine with his fucking hard-on whenever he's behind me!

GRACE

But . . . and then what? I mean, then we went into the house, and then. . . .

APRIL

And then why didn't I fight them? Why didn't I fucking fight them? Are you asking me that?

GRACE

Well. I guess so, yeah.

APRIL

There were *so many of them,* Grace! There were *so many of them!* Like eight, or six, or ten, or . . . God, I can't even remember anymore how many there were! And I thought, what if I piss them off? You know? What will they do to me? I thought, they're going to do it to me anyway. I don't know how to stop them. But I don't want them to hurt me too. I was scared they'd hurt me, stupid and scared, I was chicken. So I went along, so sue me, so sue me.

GRACE

All right, now don't get upset.

APRIL

How can I not get upset? I was counting on you! I'm still counting on you, and you turn up and you tell me—

GRACE

We're still just talking here. All we're doing right now is just talking here, so there's no need to get upset.

APRIL

Not me. I'm not just talking.

GRACE

Well. I don't know what to say.

APRIL

You have to help me.

GRACE

I'm trying to help. . . .

APRIL

No, I don't mean any pussy bullshit about exploring my feelings, I mean you have to help me, you have to support me, you have to do this with me, you have to press charges and take the stand. And you have to pay for most of the lawyer, too, and don't you dare make any snide remarks.

GRACE

I. . . .

APRIL

There's no physical evidence and it was years ago and if I go in there alone they'll just laugh at me, but with you there's a chance. . . . Grace, I don't even know if I can pay the retainer!

GRACE

How much is a retainer?

APRIL

How should I know?

GRACE

Me, neither. . . . I don't know if I can do what you want, April.

APRIL

One question. Answer one question. Did you say no? Did you ask them to stop?

GRACE

Well. . . .

APRIL

Did you fucking tell them to stop? Yes or fucking no?

GRACE

I did say those words, yes.

APRIL

And did they listen?

GRACE

They kind of laughed and said "come on." But no, I guess they didn't really listen. But more importantly, I changed my mind.

APRIL

You what?

GRACE

What, a girl can't change her mind?

APRIL

What the fuck do you mean?

GRACE

I mean, God, I mean what I'm saying. I said "no" and they laughed and said "come on" and I laughed and said "all right." How many times can I say it? How many ways? I said "no" partly to be coy, mainly to buy time because I was nervous, but I always knew I was going to go in there anyway and do them.

APRIL

You're bailing on me.

GRACE

What's the statute of limitations, anyway?

APRIL

What?

GRACE

The statute of limitations. Like, if a crime's committed, then usually there's only a certain window of time within which you can prosecute the—

APRIL

I fucking know what statute of limitations means! I'm not fucking stupid!

GRACE

Well, then, what is it?

APRIL

What, you mean for rape?

GRACE

Yeah, for rape. I mean, it *has* been more than a decade. Is it even still possible to press charges, or is all this moot?

APRIL

I, well, I mean, fuck, does it run out? For rape? I mean, rape's like murder. Isn't it?

GRACE

Surely not.

APRIL

Of course it is!

GRACE

Well, I don't know, that's why I'm asking.

APRIL

See, this is the kind of stuff I need you for, you're more sort of practical than me. . . .

GRACE

April. I don't think anybody raped me. How can I stand up and accuse someone of a thing like that if they didn't do it?

APRIL

They did.

GRACE

I don't feel like they did.

APRIL

Oh yeah? Then how do you feel? You told them to quit. They didn't quit. Four or five guys climbed on top of you and fucked you after you told them to stop. You just said yourself that afterwards you felt ashamed and filthy. But you felt like it was your fault you felt that way. Hey, let me fill you in on something: that's the way a fifteen-year-old feels when she gets raped. I know. I'm an adult, looking back at a kid. Let me tell you some other stuff about how you felt. A few minutes ago you made a big deal over not remembering how that night ended. You couldn't remember where we wound up sleeping. But you must remember that my parents had left town for the night. They told me to be good and they just took off, because this all happened before they knew I wasn't good. You told your mom and dad you were going to spend the night at my house without mentioning to them that there were no parents there, and that's where they dropped you off. Then we got *Peter* to come pick us up. After the boys were done with us, after we'd been fucked, someone turned on the TV and we all watched Jay Leno, and when it was over you asked Peter to take us both home. I remember, because it was the very first thing you'd said, after. I'd been clenching myself waiting for you to say something—I didn't think I'd ever be able to speak unless you started talking first. So I know that that was the first thing you said. Peter didn't really say anything, he just sort of grunted, but he got up and gave us a lift. None of the other guys said goodbye to us. In his car, I heard you tell him your address and say that he should drop you off first, because your house was on the way to mine. And I leaned forward—because I was in the backseat—and I asked you if you'd mind coming home with me, and staying with me, and I told you I'd like that a lot. A slumber party kind of thing, I said, a stupid thing to say. Peter laughed that stupid huh-huh laugh and made some lesbian joke. Meanwhile you said no. You wanted to be alone, you said.

GRACE

I said that?

APRIL

Yeah, you did.

GRACE

I swear I wouldn't have, if I'd realized how upset you were.

APRIL

Oh, Grace. Don't you get it? *You* were upset. For a long while I hated you for not coming over to my house. . . .

GRACE

Is that why we quit hanging out so much? Your hating me?

APRIL

So you do remember that we quit hanging out?

GRACE

I remember you mentioning it a few minutes ago.

APRIL

All right, fine. Yeah, partly that. But also . . . you'd *seen* me. Plus, I felt disgusted by you the same way I felt disgusted by myself, except since it was you and not me I could stand to think about it more. And it wasn't until years and years later that I realized that. That blaming you was just blaming myself. That you didn't come home with me because you were feeling the exact same way I was. That we were sisters. . . . If we weren't raped then I don't know what happened.

GRACE

I don't know.

APRIL

Exactly what do you not know?

GRACE

What if I just really did feel like going home, you know?

APRIL

You're hiding, Grace.

GRACE

I don't know, all right?

2 6

APRIL

What does that even mean?

GRACE

What do you think it means?

Grace rises.

APRIL

Where are you going?

GRACE

I don't know. I don't know. Let's cool down, okay? Let's, I don't know, take a break. Let's order some food or something.

APRIL

I can't really afford to get stuff delivered or eat out, I always cook. Anyway, the phone's out, remember?

GRACE

Oh, that's right. . . . Any, uh, trouble?

APRIL

Nah. I mean, not besides me not paying the bill.

GRACE

Maybe it's uncouth of me to ask, but do you need any help, April? Money help, I mean.

APRIL

Well, yeah, it is a little "uncouth," but that's fine since I don't need any money. I just forgot to mail them the check, is all, I'll do it tomorrow.

GRACE

I was only asking.

APRIL

No, I know. I guess I appreciate it. *(Pause.)* You know, I'm really not some pathetic person.

GRACE

I didn't say you were.

APRIL

Of course you didn't *say* it.

GRACE

What have I done to make you feel pathetic?

APRIL

Nothing. We're cool, I guess, as far as all that goes. I mean, I'm pissed, but not at you exactly. At least, I don't guess I am.

GRACE

That's good.

APRIL

Yeah. I haven't been like this, you know, ever since that thing. I have not. This, this is all recent.

GRACE

Yeah?

APRIL

It is, yeah. I mean, it's always bugged me. Of course it has. I've never not had nightmares, it's never not fucked up my few already-shitty relationships. But all this . . . the . . . the lately stuff. The yelling at work. The yelling at people. The cussing all the time. The forgetting the dates. The not shopping, the not leaving the house. That's all recent. Things have been coming to a head. That's why I've been praying to see you, because otherwise I was going to lose my mind. Because I need your help. Fuck, I don't want to sound like a one-joke comedian, but—

GRACE

April, listen . . . you're alone. You're alone on this.

APRIL

I . . . what?

GRACE

Look, we've discussed it. It's done. They just didn't force us.

28

APRIL

About a dozen of them. Grabbing my arm. Me saying no.

GRACE

Look, I didn't want to do it either. Okay? A big part of me
didn't. And so I felt weird too. Abused and dirty even, fine. But
if we didn't want to do it then the proper thing was to refuse,
to really refuse. I didn't because I was a dumb kid trying to be
what I thought grown-ups were. You say you didn't because
you thought they would just go ahead and beat you up and
physically force it on you anyway. But the thing is, we'll never
know, because we didn't try. And you can't prosecute someone,
no, worse, you can't ruin someone's life, you can't lose them their
job and their marriage, by standing up and accusing them of
something they might have done, maybe, if things had turned
out differently. The point is they didn't.

APRIL

I wasn't being skittish, you inhuman bitch. I wasn't letting my
fucking imagination run away with me. I knew and I know
exactly what they were going to do. Because I felt it. Haven't
you ever felt something and known it was true?

GRACE

Well. Either way. Even if I agreed then our feelings alone
wouldn't exactly win the day in court.

APRIL

I don't even want the court. Or I do, but . . . it would have been
enough. So maybe it would be impossible to prove in court, and
I could maybe swallow that. If you would just. . . . It might all
be okay, if you would just admit that it happened, and talk to
me about it. And be with me about it. I need someone here,
Grace. Something. The court was never about the jail, it was
about the people.

GRACE

But I can't be the one, April. Because it didn't happen to me.

APRIL

It did. Coward. You betrayed us, you forgot us.

GRACE

Calm down. It didn't happen to me. Please listen. Because if you want me to help you, telling you this is the only way I know to do it. You are in charge of what happens to you. That's harsh, but it's true. You are in charge. In control. If you realized that, you'd see that you don't need me. You say you didn't want to be in that orgy. Maybe neither did I. But I made it my thing. It was my thing, mine. You didn't want it and then it happened and all of a sudden you'd been raped. I didn't want it but I made myself want it. I dared myself to become a person who wanted it, and I did, and so when it happened it was *mine.* And so I've gone years without having to think about it. You— *(Pause.)* No, wait. That's not exactly what I mean. Hang on. *(Pause.)* People talk about rights being violated. But what is a right? It's just a convenient, civilized legal fiction. If it's something you really have then how come people can take it away from you without even noticing? It's obligations that are real. Rights exist in other people, obligations in yourself. If you think of yourself as nothing but a bundle of rights then as soon as people start ignoring them, you disappear. If obligations are what you are then you're always safe, because no one can take them away, and you're always free, because you can choose what they are, you. You can have obligations to yourself. . . . What I'm trying to say, is . . . wait, hang on, let me think of how to put it. . . . Frankly, I think your need for my corroboration is just as much a symptom of your submission to external circumstances, as your sense that Peter and them raped us is.

Pause.

APRIL

I haven't felt the way I do right now since that party.

GRACE

Come on. Don't be dramatic.

APRIL

What the fuck is all that? All that "external gobbledygook"? I mean, I guess you're talking like a book, but I wouldn't know for sure because I don't read fancy retarded bullshit like that.

GRACE

Maybe I can be ridiculous sometimes. But these are real things inside of me, trying to come out.

APRIL

Was all that your version of tough love? Have you decided to think that you're being all tough-love with me?

GRACE

I'm just telling you the way I see things. Hopefully it'll be some help, but I really can't say.

APRIL

Uh-huh. Well, maybe I really should listen. Maybe you really do know what's going on. Because I'll tell you one thing for sure, and that's that you sure are an awful lot smarter than me. I could only understand maybe half of what you said.

GRACE

Well, I could . . . if you'd like, I could maybe try to—

APRIL

No, no, that's cool. I think I get the main point anyway, which is that all this shit is basically my own fault.

GRACE

That's not exactly—

APRIL

Yes it is. I let it get to my head because my head's too soft. Anyway, you're probably right. I'm a human being, Grace. That's all I am. Shit happens to me sometimes. I guess it's different for you. Maybe I'm supposed to be able to stand naked in the snow and think myself warm, but I can't. You know what we call people who do do that, by the way? Crazy people.

GRACE

All right, listen—

APRIL

No, no. You listen while I try to take your advice. You ready? Here goes: my own freshly-constructed life story, my home-made reality. When we were kids I adored you. I tagged along after you everywhere because you were smarter and tougher and prettier than me, and you knew things I wanted to know, and I adored you most of all because you were kind enough to let me follow you around. We got into some pretty rough scrapes together. Then, one day in the tenth grade, you took me to a party where we both got raped. A bunch of jocks gang-banged us. We kind of quit wanting to see each other after that. I started drinking a whole bunch to handle it—I'd learned how to drink from you, that's not a dig, I'm just showing you the connections that I've made in my head—and the drinking habit got so bad that once I hit freshman year I had to drop out and now I work at a Wal-Mart, even though the booze is gone. Ever since that party it's ridiculous, every guy I see scares me fucking shitless, deep down. Even the guys I've dated, although I guess that makes sense because they were all scary assholes. And I see now that you were right about one more thing, too—I did have a made-up you in my head. Because as time went on one thing that made the other stuff bearable was the idea that I had this sister walking around out there, who'd been through the same thing, who I could call if I ever needed to yell bad enough. Or could get up the guts to. But now I see that you're not that person I remembered. And I can understand you not wanting to be. You were lucky. You pulled yourself together. You don't want to take time off. You don't want anyone back at your fancy New York job to know that you used to be just a dumb hick slut, like me. So there's just one more favor I want to ask you, and this one I don't think you'll mind: fuck off. Get the fuck out of my apartment. Or, sorry: am I being weak? Am I caving under the "external circumstances"? All right, fine. You're gone. Stay or go, you're not here. You don't exist to me. You're not even dead. You're less than smoke. You're nothing.

Pause.

GRACE

I can respect that reaction. If that's, you know. . . . (*Pause.*) Well. Look, it was good to see you again. I hope you'll let me come see you next time I come into town. *(Grace starts to leave, then pauses and turns back towards April.)* I'm sorry I wasn't enough. It's too bad Steven wasn't in town. Even if you guys hardly knew each other . . . he'd really be the one to call. Not me. . . .

APRIL

Hey, I don't want your fucking *boyfriend.*

GRACE

No, I just mean because . . . if I were going to try to change my life . . . if things ever came to a head for me . . . then he's the one I would seek out. He was always. . . . I mean, he's not like me, you know? I say things and it comes out all fucked up. It's like there's so much empty space between what people see and what I am inside that I may as well not be here at all. . . .

APRIL

What does *that* mean?

GRACE

And there was a time . . . there was this weekend when something bad happened to me, and he . . . he kind of took care of me then. . . . *(Grace gets herself back under control.)* And as for wanting to see him . . . I mean, it really doesn't bother me that he's married. I'm glad, I'm happy for him. I just wanted us to get a coffee. *(Pause.)* Well. Bye, April.

APRIL

Jesus, Grace. What is all this you're saying? . . . Stay. Let me help you.

GRACE

No, I'm fine.

APRIL

Fine? Grace, you're running around the country with nothing to look for except an ex-boyfriend you never even dated. Looking for the one weekend where you let yourself get hurt.

Oh, sweetie, stay with me. Let me help you.

GRACE
No, please. Thank you but I'm fine. I have to go now.

APRIL
(following Grace to the door)
Grace. What I said was wrong. You're real for me.

GRACE
No, I'm not.

APRIL
No, you are.

GRACE
No, please. I don't want to be, please, I can't. Goodbye. Bye.

Exit Grace. April stares at the door; then goes to it, opens it, leans out and calls after Grace:

APRIL
We may be fucked up, but we're not crazy!

BLACKOUT

SCHOOL ROMANCE

CHARACTERS:

Leslie: 19
Wendy: 37

SETTING:

A quiet dive bar in Louisiana.

Wendy leans against the bar with a drink, looking a little bored. Leslie, beer in hand, sidles up to her.

                    LESLIE
Hey.

                    WENDY
Hey.

                    LESLIE
How are you doing tonight?

                    WENDY
A little drunk.

                    LESLIE
That's the point of this place, right?

                    WENDY
I guess.

                    LESLIE
You mind if I talk to you?

                    WENDY
That's the point of this place, right?

LESLIE

Ha, I guess so. . . . *(Leslie speaks to the bartender, who we don't see.)* Hey, man. Another of whatever the lady's having. And another, uh, Bacardi 151.

WENDY

Show-off.

LESLIE

What do you mean?

WENDY

Nobody drinks Bacardi 151 except to show off.

LESLIE

I like Bacardi 151!

WENDY

Nah. You're just trying to impress me with your superhuman feat. Show-off.

LESLIE

Well. Are you impressed?

WENDY

We'll see. It depends on whether you wind up puking and rolling around on the floor.

LESLIE

Been known to happen. *(Leslie mimes having his glass refilled, and nods to the bartender.)* Thanks.

WENDY
(doing the same)

Thanks.

LESLIE

So. What's your name?

WENDY

Wendy. You're not old enough to be in here, I don't think.

LESLIE

Shhh! . . . Me and the bartender have kind of a don't-ask/don't-tell thing going on.

WENDY

All right. Besides, when I was your age it was legal to buy alcohol at eighteen in the state of Louisiana. So it would be kinda hypocritical of me to squeal on you.

LESLIE

There ya go. Anyway, I'm so used to drinking now, it'd be silly to stop me for being under-age. I just spent the summer at an oil rig out in Texas. We'd work long, long shifts. Then me and the guys would get wasted.

WENDY

Oil rig, huh? Pays pretty good, I bet.

LESLIE

Oh, yeah. And I can do it seasonally. Like, I just finished up working there all summer, but I made enough to live on for the whole school year.

WENDY

You're in school.

LESLIE

I'm gonna start over at Louisiana Tech. I didn't go last year after I graduated high school, because . . . I don't know. But now I figure I may as well.

WENDY

You may as well.

LESLIE

Ain't you gonna ask me my name?

WENDY

Already know it. Leslie.

LESLIE

How did you—. . . . First of all, I go by Mark.

WENDY

Your first name is Leslie.

LESLIE

Nobody calls me that, though. Except my mom, and dad. . . .
For real, how did you know that?

WENDY

What's wrong with "Leslie"?

LESLIE

It's a girl's name is what's wrong with it.

WENDY

Boys can be named Leslie.

LESLIE

Sure. But it's not a good idea.

WENDY

Maybe your parents were broad-minded.

LESLIE

I was named after my Uncle Leslie who died before I was born.

WENDY

Your uncle on whose side?

LESLIE

My mom's. . . . How did you know my name was Leslie?

WENDY

You look like a Leslie.

LESLIE

All right, now. . . .

WENDY

Don't get offended! . . . Anyway, I'm the one who should be
offended. Because we've met before, and yet you don't seem to
remember.

LESLIE
You know . . . I thought you did seem kinda familiar. . . .

WENDY
Oh-ho, now he says so. . . .

LESLIE
No, I did think that . . . but really dimly familiar. . . . Come on, where'd we meet?

WENDY
I've probably changed a lot. But you still look the same. Same bright face.

LESLIE
Wendy . . . Wendy . . . your face looks familiar, but I don't remember ever knowing a Wendy. . . .

WENDY
I bet if I told you my last name you'd be able to place me.

LESLIE
Well, tell me your last name then.

WENDY
I don't know. It might screw up this nice conversation we're having. Make things awkward.

LESLIE
Why would it freak me out to know your last name? Are you a famous axe murderer or something?

WENDY
Freakier. You know, it's amazing how little your face has changed. I've thought about you every once in a while, you know. Because all through those years you were probably the sweetest and most good-natured of all of them.

LESLIE
What?! Okay, come on now, how do you know me?! And more important, how do you know my first name?

WENDY

My last name is Singleton.

LESLIE

Singleton . . . Singleton. . . .

WENDY

No?

LESLIE

Wait a minute. . . . Hoooolyyyy shit. . . .

WENDY

Yup.

LESLIE

(slams the bar top)

Hey, man! Give us two more drinks! I'm sitting up in here
trying to pick up my kindergarten teacher! . . . Holy *shit!* And
you *remembered* me?! How the fuck did you *remember* me?

WENDY

I was a good teacher back then. And yours was my very first
class. I got to know all my kids pretty well, at the beginning.
And like I said, you were a very sweet, good-natured boy. And
you haven't changed. I can recognize your eyes. Your mouth.

LESLIE

Well, holy shit. . . . You still a teacher?

WENDY

No. I quit. I work at the Citgo now.

LESLIE

I've been to that gas station, I don't remember seeing you.

WENDY

I work the night shift.

LESLIE

How come you quit teaching?

WENDY

Oh, well. . . . I guess the truth is that I ran out of patience with the kids. You're supposed to keep in mind that they're not grown-ups, but I just started losing my temper all the time. Because . . . you were very sweet, but some of those other boys. . . . I know they're just little children, but still. The way they act. They're like vicious little pack animals, and they sure are brave when there's a gang of them around someone littler. . . . I couldn't teach anymore. My husband that I got married to when I was seventeen, he never hit me or anything like that. But he would just be so mean, and when his buddies came over he'd make jokes about me to them, right in front of me, and they'd laugh. Sometimes one of them would kind of shrug and say, "Come on now, Bill," but none of them would ever *do* anything about it. And then after I got divorced it was the same thing. I dated a bunch of men who treated me like garbage even though they never would have had the balls to actually hit me. They were all just vicious little childish cowards. And then I'd go to school and I'd look at those little boys, and I couldn't stand them. They all seemed like little monsters to me, miniature men. Except for the occasional one. Like you. I remember, you were always kinda innocent.

LESLIE

Innocent.

WENDY

I remember one time when some older boys, seven or eight years old, they ganged up on a kindergartener. It was this little five-year-old Asian boy who had something wrong with his mouth that made him talk funny. I think he might have been a little retarded.

LESLIE

I remember that kid, I think. Man, I haven't thought about him in forever.

WENDY

Those second- or third-graders pinned him against a wall and

41

just kind of slapped and kicked at him, and laughed at him. They didn't really hurt him, just scared him. Me and another teacher had to break it up. Then I found you sitting alone on the swing set. You were crying over how mean those big kids had been to that little boy, and because you couldn't help.

LESLIE

I don't remember that.

WENDY

I remember it.

Pause.

LESLIE

I know what you mean, I guess. About guys. I didn't always get along with other boys at school. But now it's different. I'm a man now. I like working on the rig, I like being around men. I don't mean anything gay. *(Wendy laughs.)* Well, I don't!

WENDY

You are such a teenager. You're so *young!*

LESLIE

Well. I was just saying.

WENDY

I'm not gonna think you're gay just because you're not a bitter old man-hater like me.

LESLIE

But I like women, too.

WENDY

Sure. That's probably healthy, or whatever.

LESLIE

Women are more. . . . With guys, things are more fun. They're simple. And they're kind of rough. Like, you'll wake up in the middle of the night because one of your bunkmates at the rig has snuck a hooker into the room and they've started having a big screaming fight. That's the kind of thing that happens when you're with guys.

WENDY

I always suspected.

LESLIE

But with girls . . . with women . . . things are more, they're more. . . .

WENDY

What are they, honey?

LESLIE

This is weird, man.

WENDY

What's weird?

LESLIE

This. Talking to you like this.

WENDY

Like what?

LESLIE

You know.

WENDY

We're just having a conversation in a bar. Right?

LESLIE

Yeah, but. . . . I mean, we were gonna. . . .

WENDY

Oh, you're expecting something to happen, I guess?

LESLIE

No.

WENDY

It sounds like you are.

LESLIE

No. I just meant it was weird, bumping into you like this, in a bar this way.

WENDY

Why is that weird?

LESLIE

Because, I don't know. Because I never thought of you as . . . like . . . drinking. And doing things like that.

WENDY

Really?

LESLIE

Yeah. Sure. Really.

WENDY

So when you say you're not expecting anything to happen. You mean it never occurred to you that anything might happen? . . . Or you mean that it did occur to you, but you're worried you don't have the guts?

LESLIE

The *guts?* . . . Hey, come on, Wendy, people are looking. . . .

WENDY

Who gives a fuck?

LESLIE

I just, it's weird. . . .

WENDY

What are you afraid of?

LESLIE

I, hey, I'm not afraid of anything, okay?! Maybe you're just a little old!

WENDY

Ah. Okay.

LESLIE

Look . . . I'm sorry, but. . . .

WENDY

I'm not old, you dumb teenager. I'm, like, thirty-seven.

LESLIE

Well . . . I'm nineteen.

WENDY

You didn't think I was too old to walk up to, five minutes ago.

LESLIE

Well . . . the light in here is dim. . . .

WENDY

Oh, so now that you're close up you can see what a withered old crone I am?

LESLIE

No . . . actually, no . . . you're really good-looking, up close . . . you're beautiful, actually . . . it's just, it's weird. . . .

Pause.

WENDY

Little vicious pack animals. Little cowards. *(Pause.)* The thing about you was that even though you had friends and all, you still liked to go off by yourself. Most of the kids who would wander off alone, it was because the others chased them off. Or else the other kids would mark them out as weird loners and would pick on them for that reason. But you managed to have it both ways. They would let you go off by yourself and not mess with you. It was because you had such a nice face. *(Pause.)* You know I hit a kid once?

LESLIE

Is that how come you quit teaching?

WENDY

I didn't get fired or anything, if that's what you mean. No

45

one knew. I lost my temper and I slapped this little boy. This kindergartener. It wasn't hard enough to leave a mark, because even as I hit him I was pulling back. You know what I mean? Part of me hit him and part of me was yanking my hand back. So it wound up being this little smack across his cheek. We were alone in the room, I'd held him after the other kids had been taken out to recess by the student teacher. I couldn't believe I'd hit him. As soon as I did it, I told him that he was never to tell anyone. I was very stern. I still figured that as soon as he got home he'd spill it to his mom and dad and that'd be that. I couldn't sleep that night, all during the drive to school the next morning I figured I'd find the principal waiting for me at the door. Along with maybe some cops. But, no. I guess that little boy never told anybody. He stayed pretty quiet for the rest of the year, too. Brian. His name was Brian.

LESLIE

Why did you hit him?

WENDY

He was a smart-ass kid. He was just a smart-ass little kid. I mean, that wasn't all of it, obviously. I was dating this asshole named Ray at the time, and he was making me crazy, and I guess I took it out on the kids.

LESLIE

What did he do, Ray?

WENDY

Nothing worth me getting so upset over. Stupid stuff! Like, the day before I hit Brian, we were in his truck together, out on the highway in the middle of the woods. We were arguing. And I was right—I mean, it was a dumb-ass argument that we were having, but still, I was in the right, and he was just being stubborn. So I said something like, "You're so full of shit. You know I'm right and you're wrong and you just aren't man enough to say so." Well, he slowed down the truck and then pulled over to the side of the road. "What're you doing?," I wanted to know. "Giving you a chance to cool down," he said. He got out of the truck, took the keys and his gun with him, and slipped off into the woods. I figured he'd just stopped to go to the bathroom. But then he didn't come back. I waited there alone while the big rigs zoomed by. I sat there an hour stewing, and by then my pride was broken down enough for me to open the truck door and holler into the woods for Ray. But no answer. . . . I don't know how long went by in all. It felt like forever, but when he came back to the truck the sun hadn't gone down yet. . . . I guess really he didn't do anything, just walked into the woods. But when he came back, the way he was smirking. . . . I just felt humiliated. The way I'd sat in the cab of that truck, waiting like a good little woman for him to come back! I wished so much that I'd gone into the woods to hunt for him, or hitchhiked out, or tried to hitchhike . . . anything but just sitting there, waiting so obediently for him to come back. . . . I went to bed that night seething, I woke up the next morning seething, I went to class seething. And I wound up slapping Brian in the face.

LESLIE
That guy Ray sounds like a real asshole.

WENDY
He was a real asshole.

LESLIE
You ever see him around anymore?

WENDY
Of course. He was born around here, he's lived around here his whole life, he'll die around here. I bump into him at the Wal-Mart or the gas station. No one ever leaves. Except for you, I guess, with your oil rig.

LESLIE
I like to leave. Go see someplace new. Even if it is just the middle of nowhere in Texas.

WENDY
They always say, "Aw, they're just kids." When I started teaching that's what I said, whenever they got on my nerves. But then as the years went by I would think, "Well, aren't they

kids who will grow up to be assholes? So what if they're small, if they act exactly the same as the full-grown animals?" . . . That day, little Brian was acting like such a little bastard. And the smirk on his face, it looked just like the smirk on Ray's when he came out of those woods and knew he'd made me worry and embarrassed me and pissed me off. And I thought how good it would feel to slap that smirk right off his little face. And then I did slap it off, and it did feel good. But I used to love kids, in the beginning.

LESLIE
What was the fight about? That you had with that guy?

WENDY
It was nothing.

LESLIE
But do you remember it?

WENDY
Yes. I remember it. But it was stupid.

LESLIE
Sure it was stupid, most fights are stupid. But what was it?

WENDY
It was about whether or not Kirstie Alley was the first one on "Cheers," or whether it was that other woman, the one who played Diane. Ray thought Kirstie Alley came first. . . . I couldn't believe it! We'd watched the show together! I mean, it didn't matter, but he was so sure Kirstie Alley had been on the show first! . . .

LESLIE
What's "Cheers"?

WENDY
What?

LESLIE
What's "Cheers"?

WENDY

It's a TV show. It's, like, one of the most popular sitcoms of all time. What year were you born, anyway?

LESLIE

1990.

WENDY

Jesus. . . . Well. . . . It doesn't matter. It's just a sitcom. It wasn't important enough to remember. Even if I did slap a five-year-old's face over it.

LESLIE

Yeah, but that was over other stuff . . . not that. . . .

WENDY

May as well have been over that. . . . When I started out I loved kids. But then I just got ruined. Being lonely all the time and being stuck around here. My parents and my brother are still here. We hardly ever talk but it isn't like I have anyone anywhere else. I don't have any money to move anywhere. I don't know how to do anything. I could never teach again, I couldn't stand it. I just work in the gas station.

LESLIE

Come on. You could figure something out.

WENDY

You think that because you're so young. Do you know my tits started sagging when I was only thirty? That early? I turned thirty and I've been an old lady ever since.

LESLIE

Wendy . . . come on . . . maybe stop drinking now. . . .

WENDY

You are lucky. You know that? To get to go off someplace. . . .

LESLIE

Sometimes I wish the opposite . . . I wish I could go back . . . back to. . . . *(Pause.)* Never mind. I don't know what I'm talking about.

WENDY

Get out of here. You were right. This is weird. I remember you crying when your momma dropped you off, for Christ's sake. I shouldn't be letting you chat me up in a bar.

LESLIE

You don't remember that. How could you remember that?

WENDY

Maybe I'm a genius. . . . Go on, get out of here. You're making me feel like I really am old.

Pause. Wendy looks away. Leslie hesitates, then moves up behind her. He gently takes her by the waist, pulls her back against him. Wendy closes her eyes and lets him do so. Leslie puts his mouth to her ear and whispers.

LESLIE

Ms. Singleton. . . .

Wendy turns in his arm, puts her face to his; they kiss. As they kiss, she rotates so that they're face-to-face, and she embraces him. Coming out of the kiss, they smile at each other, and their mood is light and playful.

WENDY

Do you wanna go on a field trip, honey?

LESLIE

Yes, ma'am.

WENDY

Do you have a permission slip from your mommy and daddy?

LESLIE

Gosh, I'm sorry, I just didn't feel like telling them where I was going.

WENDY

Uh-oh. Well, what are we going to do with you, then?

LESLIE

You could punish me.

WENDY

Nah. I don't think so. You seem like such a good boy.

LESLIE

Am I a good boy? You think so?

WENDY

I think so. But we'll see. Now, are you gonna mind me?

LESLIE

Yes, ma'am.

WENDY

You gonna do everything I say?

LESLIE

Cross my heart and hope to die.

Pause.

WENDY

It'll be nice. To teach again.

They kiss.

BLACKOUT

PART II

PORNOPHILES

CHARACTERS:

Preston: 20's, or early 30's. Miranda's boyfriend.
Miranda: 20's, or early 30's. Pretty. Socialite. Always on the move. Preston's girlfriend.

The stage needs nothing more than a couple of chairs, or possibly a loveseat.

The lights come up; Preston is wringing his hands, pacing, nervous about something. Enter Miranda, obviously in a hurry.

MIRANDA
So what's this big discussion that you want to have with me? . . . I don't have much time, I've got to get ready for the foundation's benefit tonight.

PRESTON
It's kind of hard for me to say this, Miranda.

MIRANDA
Well, it's a little hard for me to just stand around if you're not going to talk, Preston. I have a lot of work to do.

PRESTON
Please. I feel a little nervous.

MIRANDA
Around *me?* *(Suddenly she seems to guess what this is all about. She moves closer to Preston.)* Preston. Darling. Whatever it is, just go ahead. Just say it.

PRESTON
Well. . . . It's about your sister. . . .

MIRANDA

My sister? It's about Gillian? Oh. . . .

PRESTON

What's wrong?

MIRANDA

It's just . . . no, nothing, it's silly. . . .

PRESTON

What is it?

MIRANDA

It's stupid. I guess I thought maybe you wanted to . . . I don't know . . . finally ask me to marry you. . . .

PRESTON

Oh, honey. . . . Have we not been through all that before?

MIRANDA

All right, so I thought I'd worn down your resistance!

PRESTON

I just . . . I've told you, marriage to me feels like such a fakey, old-fashioned ritual. I love you, but the thought of standing up in front of all those people, and saying those words in public, those super-formal words . . . all the pomp and circumstance . . . it just makes me feel silly. . . .

MIRANDA

All right. Now that we've gotten my schoolgirlish hopes and dreams disposed of, I've got some work to do. . . .

PRESTON

Wait, Miranda, I still want to talk. . . .

MIRANDA

Gillian will be at the benefit, so maybe afterwards we can include her in the conversation. . . .

PRESTON

God! Can't your stupid benefit wait five minutes?

Preston immediately regrets having called the benefit "stupid." He eyes Miranda warily; she fixes a deadly look upon him.

MIRANDA

Not really. My family's been doing important work with this charity for fifty years. That brings meaning to my life. Which is more than is likely to happen with my relationship, it looks like. So if you'll excuse me. . . .

PRESTON

Miranda, I think we really should talk about Gillian!

Miranda hears something worrisome in his voice.

MIRANDA

Is something really wrong?

PRESTON

Maybe we'd better sit down.

MIRANDA

My God, what is it? Has something happened? Is she all right?

PRESTON

It's nothing you need to worry too much about, honey. But . . . well, yes, I suppose it is serious. Or at least, it's something that . . . well, it's an issue that I feel you should know about.

MIRANDA

My God. Well, don't keep me in suspense.

PRESTON

I don't want to seem like I'm sticking my nose into your family's business.

MIRANDA

Have we ever made you feel like an outsider?

PRESTON

No. Not really. But I know that by your family's standards I'm a little . . . well . . . rough around the edges. Not that I haven't always been treated with respect, and I'm grateful for that. But your family's pedigree . . . it can be a bit intimidating.

MIRANDA
Preston. If there's something that needs to be resolved between us, please, tell me what it is and we'll resolve it. But if there's something that involves my little sister—something bad— please, tell me what that thing is first.

PRESTON
All right. You're right, you're right. I just, I don't want to be perceived as speaking against your family.

MIRANDA
Preston. . . .

PRESTON
And the worst thing is, well, I'm afraid of making myself look shabby in *your* eyes, on top of everything else—on top of causing you grief. . . . I'm telling you, I almost couldn't bear that.

MIRANDA
Preston. . . .

PRESTON
All right, all right. Well, Gillian is . . . I mean, as you know, Gillian is a . . . is a *confused* girl. . . .

MIRANDA
(laughing)
Well, after all, she's *only* twenty-seven. . . .

PRESTON
. . . She's a girl who has certain, well, self-*esteem* issues. . . .

MIRANDA
Now you've lost me. I sometimes feel like she could do with a bit *less* self-esteem.

PRESTON
But you know what I mean. Didn't you tell me yourself that you used to call her Junk-in-the-Trunk?

MIRANDA
Oh my God. What should I say? Sisters can be cruel.

PRESTON
But don't be too hard on yourself. After all, there *is* an element of truth to it.

MIRANDA
What do you mean?! Gillian is a perfectly attractive girl!

PRESTON
Oh, *yeah,* she's attractive! What I'm saying is that I saw her . . . I . . . I mean . . . uh. . . .

MIRANDA
You saw her? You saw her *where?*

PRESTON
I . . . uh . . . well. . . .

MIRANDA
Preston. Did you see Gillian someplace in particular? Someplace other than here, or at Mother's and Father's, or at the country club?

PRESTON
I . . . uh . . . jeez. *(Preston comes to Miranda, takes her hand.)* Miranda. Have you ever heard of something called www.assparade.com?

MIRANDA
www.assparade.com?

PRESTON
Yes.

MIRANDA
It sounds like a website.

PRESTON
It is a website, yes.

MIRANDA
What kind of a website is it?

PRESTON

Miranda. I think it's sort of self-explanatory what kind of a website it is.

MIRANDA

I guess it's not about parades.

PRESTON

No, not the regular kind.

MIRANDA

May I assume that this is a change of subject, and that we aren't talking about my little sister anymore?

PRESTON

I'm, uh, afraid not, Miranda.

MIRANDA

So when you say that you *saw* my little sister. . . .

PRESTON

Yes, my dear.

MIRANDA

. . . you mean that you *saw* her . . .

PRESTON

It's true, my love.

MIRANDA

Oh, *ugh!* That little *whore!*

PRESTON

Now, don't say . . . or, well, yeah, okay.

MIRANDA

That . . . *ugh!* How *could* she? I mean, has she run through her trust fund *already?!*

PRESTON

Darling, I don't think it's for the money.

MIRANDA
Oh, so you're saying that my sister is a freak? Like one of those girls in the *rap* videos!

PRESTON
No, no, no, but it's just . . . I mean, I think that Gillian may need our support. Maybe it's some sort of body-image thing.

MIRANDA
Oh! So you're saying that this is *my* fault! Because I used to call her Junk-in-the-Trunk!

PRESTON
No, no. . . .

MIRANDA
Sisters do that kind of thing, Preston! That's just what sisters do!

PRESTON
I wasn't trying to blame *you* in particular! But there's a whole sociocultural complex that pushes young women into this sort of thing.

MIRANDA
Ugh. . . . I suppose maybe you're right. I have to admit, it doesn't exactly make it less upsetting to know that *you* saw *her,* doing *that.*

PRESTON
It will make things awkward at the benefit.

MIRANDA
Wait a minute.

PRESTON
Yes, dear?

MIRANDA
Preston?

PRESTON
Yes?

61

MIRANDA

How did *you* come across . . . what was it called?

PRESTON

You mean www.assparade.com?

MIRANDA

Yes, that one, the assparade.com.

PRESTON

Oh, I just, you know . . . was surfing the web. . . .

MIRANDA

Surfing the web? What did you google?

PRESTON

Uh . . . I googled . . . assparade. . . .

MIRANDA

I see. I didn't realize your tastes ran that way.

PRESTON

You didn't know I like *ass?*

MIRANDA

Is there anything I can do to make myself more pleasing to you?
Any special fatty diets you'd like me to take up? Any exercises
you'd like me to stop doing?

PRESTON

Now, now, honey, please. . . .

MIRANDA

Maybe I should watch my sister on-line, see if I can pick up any
pointers.

PRESTON

Honey, no. It's just . . . sometimes, when you're working late
at the foundation and I'm here alone, I get . . . well . . . lonely.

MIRANDA

I thought you were slaving away at your painting.

PRESTON

Well. Not *slaving*.

MIRANDA

This is good. This is educational. I guess it can't hurt, picking up little tidbits about your boyfriend's psyche like this. . . .

PRESTON

Oh, Miranda, for God's sake, I watched a porno! I mean, we've had an internet connection in the house for years! Don't pretend you didn't know that something like this had to be going on.

MIRANDA

Hmph. Well. So tell me more. About Gillian's little hobby.

PRESTON

Oh, Miranda, please. I thought this was something you should know, but going into the details of it with you makes me feel icky.

MIRANDA

Well, buck up! . . . This website, is it popular?

PRESTON

Fairly popular, I would assume.

MIRANDA

Where do they make these things? These little movies?

PRESTON

My impression is that they're filmed locally.

MIRANDA

How can you tell? Surely they have the decency to make these videos behind closed doors! Or does your kind get off watching people hump in front of national landmarks?

PRESTON

I only meant that it seems logical to suppose they're made here, since Gillian is here and she's also in the videos, so one would logically think they were in the same place.

MIRANDA

I don't know, what with all the gallivanting she does. For instance, come summer she's in Miami every other weekend.

PRESTON

That's true. When I bumped into her on the set, I was so shocked that at first I tried to make light of it all by asking her if she was earning pocket money for her air fare.

MIRANDA

Wait a second. On the set?

PRESTON

Um.

MIRANDA

You mean that after you stumbled across this video of Gillian, you tracked down the people who made it, and went down there, and saw Gillian actually on the set at this assparade.com?

PRESTON

Um.

MIRANDA

So you've already confronted her about it?

PRESTON

Um.

MIRANDA

And you've confronted her *on the set?* . . . Wait a second . . . *on* the *set.* . . .

Miranda gasps, stares at Preston accusatorily.

PRESTON

Now please, my love, don't get excited. . . .

MIRANDA

You *whore!*

PRESTON

Miranda—I've told you before that it hurts me when you say things like that.

MIRANDA

It hurts *me* when you screw my sister and post the video on the internet.

PRESTON

No no no, you're jumping to conclusions. We haven't actually been paired up yet.

MIRANDA

Ugh!

PRESTON

Miranda. I know you're upset, but *please*. Let's not forget who we are! We're open-minded! We're not red-state people!

MIRANDA

You little whore. I picked you up out of the gutters of suburban New Jersey. Have you forgotten where I found you? Hawking your canvases at the craft fair for fifteen dollars a pop. I lifted you out of all that. I brought you to this mansion and I knocked down a wall and converted two guest bedrooms into a studio for you. I introduced you to gallery owners and I invited you into a family with a pedigree as long as . . . as long as . . . as long as anybody *else's* around here. And all that wasn't enough for you? You have to go moonlighting as a porn . . . what? Porn star or extra?

PRESTON

Star.

MIRANDA

Fine, a porn star. Well, I hope the pay is really good. I hope it's worth more than all this. Worth more than me.

PRESTON

Oh, Miranda, don't you know that you're the love of my life! But that's not what this is about. . . . Of course I appreciate all that you've done for me. But all these days and nights here alone, alone with myself and my paintings, while you're at the foundation, busy helping others . . . well, it got to me. And assparade was a chance for me to be a part of something bigger than myself, and to do something with other people! With a *lot* of other people!

MIRANDA
I guess I'm a prude.

PRESTON
Oh, please, Miranda. Come off it.

MIRANDA
Ex*cuse* me?!

PRESTON
I love you, Miranda—I really do. And I want to spend the rest of my life with you. But I don't know if that's going to happen if you keep setting yourself above me in these artificial ways.

MIRANDA
You were naked in a room with my sister on the set of www.assparade.com.

PRESTON
I'm not saying that I haven't made mistakes. And maybe at heart I am just another one of the bridge-and-tunnel crowd. . . .

MIRANDA
More like tunnel than bridge, I'd say.

PRESTON
What?

MIRANDA
Nothing. It was just, I was just trying to make a joke, is all. . . .

PRESTON
I don't get it.

MIRANDA
No, don't worry, it was a really stupid joke. . . .

PRESTON
No, I didn't mean to call you stupid, I just didn't get it. . . .

MIRANDA

It was just a really dumb, really tacky joke. . . . Like, as in, a "tunnel" is kind of like a . . . like a you-know-what. . . .

PRESTON

I don't. . . . Oh! . . . Oh, my. . . .

MIRANDA

Can we please just forget my stupid joke and go on with what you were saying?

PRESTON

I was going to say that, I know it's probably unintentional. I know what a loving person you are. But you can sometimes give the impression of being sort of elitist and holier-than-thou.

MIRANDA

Oh I can, can I.

PRESTON

Like I said, I know that's not the real you. I feel like you're over-compensating for some kind of feeling of inferiority. Or like there's something inside you that you feel you can't show the rest of the world. Something that you've got to hide, something soft and vulnerable. And so you pull this porcupine act.

MIRANDA

Well. I may not share your peccadilloes. But I'm definitely not an elitist.

PRESTON

It's not just me who thinks so, Miranda.

MIRANDA

Oh, really?

PRESTON

Your family agrees.

MIRANDA

Liar. When have you been talking to my family?

PRESTON

I talk to your family. How would you know? You're never around. Always at your damned foundation.

MIRANDA

So when did you all have this big bull session about me behind my back?

PRESTON

It wasn't behind your *back,* you just happened not to *be* there. The other day, after we'd finished shooting, Gillian, your father, and I were all really hungry, so we went to this diner. . . .

MIRANDA

Wait a minute. My father was there? What was he doing at this set?

PRESTON

Oh, shit. . . .

MIRANDA

Had he come for Gillian?

PRESTON

(misunderstanding)
No, no! Not for his own *daughter!*

MIRANDA

My *father?!*

PRESTON

A lot of people do it, honey, it's very rewarding!

MIRANDA

My sister, my boyfriend, my father, who *else?* My *mother?*

PRESTON

Are you really asking?

MIRANDA

Oh my *God.* Oh, *ugh.*

PRESTON

Look, honey, I mean . . . a *lot* of people do it! Just go on the internet and see! There are all these thousands and thousands of websites, and who do you think fills them with content? Well, *somebody's* got to step up!

MIRANDA

I think maybe I should be alone for a while.

PRESTON

Honey. Don't you think you're not quite being honest with me? Is it really true, that you can't see why someone would want to be a porn star?

Pause.

MIRANDA

No, I . . . I'm not being completely honest with you. *(Pause.)* I've never been completely honest with you. *(She turns to face him, haughtily; maybe she even gives her hair a regal flip.)* The truth is that I know about these websites. I know them very well.

PRESTON

Oh, honey . . . do you mean? . . .

MIRANDA

My professional name is Mariah.

PRESTON

Mariah, you don't know how I've dreamed of hearing you say this.

MIRANDA

All those late nights at the foundation. . . . Truth is, I may be on the board but it's pretty much an honorary position. I've never spent much time worrying over the day-to-day operations of the foundation. No—I spend my evenings doing a very different kind of work.

PRESTON

You can tell me all about it. This is a safe place.

MIRANDA

I suppose I don't know why I've always wanted to keep that part of my life hidden from you all—from you, from Father and Mother, from Gillian. Why I've never wanted to show you that face. But now you know.

PRESTON

My love. Do you really think that I didn't know?

MIRANDA

You mean? . . .

PRESTON

Think back over our conversation. Do you really believe I'm so stupid as to make those blundering disclosures on accident? No. It was all a ploy, to see if you'd at last tell me what I've known all along.

MIRANDA

But how? . . .

PRESTON

I loved you before I ever met you, Mariah. I loved you from afar. I watched your videos again and again—in fact it was you who inspired me to hope to make my own videos someday. I tracked you down, learned your legal name. I tailed you—you never saw me. When I found that you frequented that crafts market I taught myself to paint. Just so I could have something to sell you.

MIRANDA

That . . . is so. . . .

They embrace.

PRESTON

Listen. Mariah. This feeling that I have . . . it's so strong. . . .

MIRANDA

For me, too.

70

PRESTON

And I love you so much that I . . . I want to make it official.
I want to share it with everyone.

MIRANDA

You mean? . . .

PRESTON

I want to make a public statement of our love. In front of
everybody, in front of the whole world.

MIRANDA

Oh, Preston, are you sure?

PRESTON

Will you make a video with me, Mariah?

MIRANDA

Oh, Preston. Yes, of course I will, yes.

They kiss.

BLACKOUT

SIBLING RIBALDRY

CHARACTERS:

Penny: 30ish. Toby's girlfriend.
Frankie: 30ish. Toby's sister.
Toby: 30ish. Penny's boyfriend, Frankie's brother.

Penny is passed out in a chair, an empty whisky bottle on the floor beside her, her limp hand still holding it lightly; she's in a white tank top covered in blood and has blood on her hands and arms. Enter Frankie.

FRANKIE
Toby? Toby?! *(She sees Penny, notices and is startled by the fact that she is covered in blood.)* Oh!

The exclamation rouses Penny, who wakes groggily and freezes as she looks over and sees Frankie.

PENNY
Oh. Uh. Hey, Frankie. You just hanging out?

FRANKIE
I was coming by to check on Toby, and . . . the door was open. . . . I knocked first, but nobody answered. . . .

PENNY
Yeah, guess I'm kind of wiped out. Whew! Hell of a weekend!

FRANKIE
Yeah . . . I . . . I tried calling, but. . . . I couldn't reach him. . . .

PENNY
He probably had his ringer off. It's been a big weekend, like I said.

FRANKIE

I was worried about him.

PENNY

Frankie—no offense, but you are a worrywart. Your brother's fine. He's just in the bedroom.

FRANKIE

I'm going to check on him. . . .

PENNY

No!

FRANKIE

Why not?!

PENNY

Because he's sleeping, is why! . . . Okay, listen, I know you and Toby have this super-intense sibling bond that's very special and that I can never hope to understand, *but*. It's a little codependent. Toby is a grown man and, in my humble opinion, you need to learn to not panic every time you go a couple days without hearing from him. Not that my opinion would count for anything, even if he *is* my boyfriend. But I happen to pay half the rent on this house. So when it comes to you marching in without knocking and wanting to wake people up from their naps, I do have some say about that.

FRANKIE

I . . . I knocked. . . .

PENNY

So nobody answers and you just charge in?! What if we didn't answer because we were having sex in the living room?!

FRANKIE

Ew! Please, that's my brother you're talking about!

PENNY

Well! He's my boyfriend! And this is our place!

FRANKIE

I just need to check on him. . . .

Frankie starts to move off-stage towards the bedroom; Penny blocks her.

PENNY

Are you not listening to me?

FRANKIE

Penny . . . are you okay?

PENNY

Don't try to turn this around on me.

FRANKIE

I just meant because you're all covered in blood.

PENNY

What? *(Penny looks down at herself; she'd forgotten she was covered in blood. She laughs, to buy time.)* Guess I forgot to change my clothes.

FRANKIE

Did you hurt yourself?

PENNY

Oh, no, don't worry, it's not my blood.

FRANKIE

Well . . . how did you get all covered in blood, Penny?

PENNY

Well, um. . . . *(Unable to think of a reason, she draws herself up with great dignity.)* You know, this is my place and I can wear what I want. This shirt may not look like much but it's comfortable.

FRANKIE

What?! How did it get all that blood on it?!

PENNY

Well, you know . . . this is an old shirt, and . . . it's been through a lot. . . .

FRANKIE

Penny, I am going to go check on my brother.

PENNY

And I'm telling you, now, while it's just you and me, woman-to-woman, and your big brother isn't here to stick up for you: it's time you learned some boundaries.

FRANKIE

If you don't let me see Toby right this second, I'm going to call the police.

PENNY

Wha. . . . You think that. . . ?

FRANKIE

That's right! There's no telling what you could have done to him!

PENNY

I *love* Toby!

FRANKIE

Yeah, but you're sick! Maybe I do check in! Maybe I do worry! But only since he started going with *you!* He changed after he met you!

PENNY

You're damn right I changed him! I released him inside! I freed him from the inhibitions that you and his—

FRANKIE

Ugh, I don't want to hear all this *trash!* I just want to see my brother! . . . Listen—either you tell me why you're bloody, or let me see Toby, or I'm calling the police.

PENNY

Okay okay okay. Just sit down, will you? I'll tell you where the blood came from. I just didn't want to at first because it's . . . well . . . a little embarrassing.

FRANKIE

Embarrassing?

PENNY

Yeah. See . . . see, this is deer blood.

FRANKIE

Deer blood?

PENNY

I hit a deer when I was out driving in, you know. The woods.

FRANKIE

You don't have a car.

PENNY

Exactly! That's part of what made it so embarrassing. And awful. See, I had borrowed a friend's car, and that was what I was driving when I hit the deer. Well, naturally, I'd sworn that I'd get the car back to her in just the same condition it was in when I picked it up. But now here I am in the woods and the car's covered with this deer that's just busted like a water balloon. So I had to clean it off the car. And also put it out of its suffering. And its little, uh, you know, little hooves, and its little horns or whatever, antlers, they were all stuck in the grill. So I had to saw them off with my Bowie knife—

FRANKIE

What, you just happened to have a Bowie knife?

PENNY

(innocently pulling out a Bowie knife to prove she has one)
Oh, I always have a Bowie knife on me, that part's completely true.

FRANKIE

Okay.

PENNY

So, like I was saying, to be able to clean the car I had to be able to get this deer off it, so I had to saw its legs out of the grill, so I got all this blood on me. And I had to saw its horns, I mean its antlers, I had to saw them out too, which . . . I mean, I guess there's not much blood in those, but, uh, you know, it's . . . it's really hard. Which is why I was passed out when you got here! From exhaustion. Also I'd been drinking! Because of the, the, the emotional strain.

FRANKIE

The car must have been practically totaled, though. If you had to disentangle the deer from it like that.

PENNY

Yeah, well. In hindsight I guess cleaning it wasn't such a pressing concern.

FRANKIE

Oh my God. I can't believe this is happening.

PENNY

It blew my mind too.

FRANKIE

You killed my brother.

PENNY

Uh. Is your brother a deer?

FRANKIE

I'm going to the police.

PENNY
(reaching out to restrain Frankie)
Now wait just a—

FRANKIE

Don't touch me! . . . I've always gotten a weird vibe off of you. I've always know you were sick. Now I don't know what's going on here. I pray it's not what I think it is. But all I know is that nothing, *nothing,* that happens in this house would surprise me.

Enter Toby, his shirt, hands and arms covered in blood.

TOBY

Hey, guys, what's going on?

FRANKIE

Toby!

TOBY

I was asleep, woke up, heard you guys talking, thought I'd come join you.

PENNY

Frankie and me were just bonding.

FRANKIE

This is weird.

TOBY

You mean me and Penny living together? Frankie, I know it can feel weird when family dynamics change. I know that, what with me and Penny having such a special bond, you're scared that maybe you're going to be replaced. But, Frankie, you will always be my baby sister.

FRANKIE

No, it's weird that you're also covered in blood.

TOBY

(looking down at himself and noticing that fact)
Oh! . . . Uh . . . yeah, I guess that's weird too. . . .

FRANKIE

Are you okay?

TOBY

Sure, of course.

FRANKIE

Well how did you get all that blood all over you?

TOBY

From, um. Uh. Cooking.

FRANKIE

From *cooking?!*

TOBY

Yeah, sure, from cooking.

FRANKIE

From cooking *what?!*

PENNY

Deer!

TOBY

Yeah, Penny's uncle brought over this deer that he shot and he gave it to us.

FRANKIE

He gave you a whole deer?

TOBY

Sure. But it still had all its skin and hair and eyes and stuff, so we had to, what's it called, skin and dress it. Hence the blood.

FRANKIE

You don't know how to skin and dress a deer!

TOBY

On-line tutorial.

PENNY

Yeah, we found this great on-line tutorial, with videos and everything. . . .

FRANKIE

I thought you said you hit the deer with your car? Now all of a sudden your uncle bagged it?

PENNY

Baby, I couldn't bear to tell you about the accident, it was too horrible.

TOBY

You *lied* to me!

FRANKIE

Enough, enough, *enough!* Enough *bullshit!* Penny, could you excuse me and my brother for a minute? *(Penny makes a big point of walking up to Toby and Frankie and standing only a foot away, staring at the two of them; Frankie rolls her eyes, turns back to Toby.)* Listen, Toby. I have this friend who had a friend who knew a guy who was going to MIT. Now, this guy was really smart, and there was nothing wrong with him. Just like you! But Scientologists got hold of him. At first his friends didn't worry too much—they were like, Okay, you've got a right to whatever weird opinion or lifestyle you want, just like everyone else. But then things gradually intensified. And you know what wound up happening? They wound up having to tie him up and lock him in his room because otherwise he was going to give all of his money away to the Scientologists. And I think something like that's happened to you.

PENNY
Excuse me. Do I look like a fucking Scientologist to you?

FRANKIE
You've been brainwashed or something, or . . . or I don't know what! But something's going on, Toby! You've changed somehow, there's something different about you since you hooked up with this, this *person!* I can't put my finger on it, but there is!

TOBY
Wait. Okay, okay, this is ridiculous. I'll explain.

FRANKIE
Yeah? *Really?*

TOBY
Really. You see, Frankie, Penny and I love each other very much. We really were made for each other. Now, sometimes, the way you can tell that the person you're in love with really was made especially for you, is because they . . . *share* things with you. Say, for example, that they share some particular ideas with you. Or some need, say. Some emotional need. Now, Penny and I—

PENNY
Wait wait wait. You're not going to *tell* her, are you? *Really* tell her?

81

TOBY

Yes.

PENNY

Are you crazy?!

TOBY

Maybe. I'm not sure.

PENNY

She has no right to know this stuff about us, Toby!

TOBY

Penny, I'm sorry if it doesn't seem fair to you or if it's hard for you to understand. But Frankie's concerned, and her concerns are legitimate, and I do feel an obligation to address them.

PENNY

But this is *my personal sexual shit* we're talking about! Our sex life belongs to *me, too,* you know? This is *my personal weird shit!*

TOBY

Penny, baby—please try to understand.

PENNY

Oh, well. Don't let little old me stop you from doing what's right. . . .

Penny stalks in disgust to a far corner of the stage.

TOBY

Well, Frankie. There's not a day goes by that I don't get down on my knees and thank the Universe for having sent me Penny. Because it turns out that in addition to all the other wonderful stuff about her, we also have this . . . well, there's this thing that we share, this requirement, this connection, which is . . . uh. . . . Okay. For both of us, in order to consummate the act of physical love, we have to, uh, we have to, kill. A person. Like, in order to climax, we have to kill a person together.

FRANKIE

Kill someone.

TOBY

Yeah. But, Frankie, I hope you'll be able to look past this and see that I'm still your big brother Toby, just like I've always been.

FRANKIE

I guess I was imagining that you were going to explain that you *hadn't* killed anyone.

TOBY

Well. You see that we're both covered in blood.

FRANKIE

(turning away from Toby and Penny, walking a bit up-stage)
I . . . I know you're still my brother, Toby, but I'm not sure I can accept this.

TOBY

Don't turn your back on me, Frankie.

During Frankie's speech, behind her back, Penny sidles up to Toby and begins whispering in his ear, trying to persuade him of something. Her manner is seductive, cajoling. At first Toby resists whatever it is that she's saying, but she presses; as the conversation progresses Toby periodically looks over uncertainly at Frankie, his resolve wavering; Penny runs her fingers through his hair; by the time Frankie finishes her speech Toby has come around to Penny's view of things—which, of course, is that Frankie should be their next victim. Frankie doesn't have any idea any of this is happening.

FRANKIE

I'll never abandon you, Toby. Not really. But. . . . No. It's not that I don't forgive you. But I can't stand by while you kill people—even if it *is* just to satisfy your sexual desires. I don't know if you'll be able to understand this, but it's because I love you that I have to turn you in. See, it's hard for me to explain, but . . . in order for the love I feel for you to mean anything, then life itself has to have meaning. I mean, *some* kind of meaning, even if I don't necessarily know what it is. And if I just walk out of here and let you go on letting Penny talk you into all these massacres, then I'll always feel like life is meaningless. And then love will be meaningless, too. . . . God, I sound stupid, I know I'm not making any sense. Anyway, I'm going to the police, Toby, I'm turning you in. I have faith that one day you'll understand, even if you don't right now. *(She turns to leave. Toby blocks her way)* Toby? Come on, don't make this harder, please get out of the way. *(She turns to walk the other direction. Penny blocks her.)* Come on! *(Penny and Toby exchange a significant, intense gaze—comprehension dawns on Frankie—Penny takes out her Bowie knife, advances towards Frankie—Frankie backs away.)* You guys are both totally disgusting.

BLACKOUT

A BEAUTIFUL CIRCLE OF LOVE AND ACCEPTANCE

CHARACTERS:

Graham
Phil
Tracy

Graham and Phil are standing nervously in a room. Graham seems more freaked out, Phil more embarrassed.

GRAHAM
Do you think she seemed mad?

PHIL
Well, I don't know her that well. . . .

GRAHAM
But what did you think?!

PHIL
She *seemed* mad, yes. . . .

GRAHAM
What do you think she's going to do?

PHIL
I don't know, Graham. You're the one who lives with her.

GRAHAM
Yeah, but you're the one who's dating her.

PHIL

This is our first date. Or was. I guess this part of the evening doesn't count as a date anymore.

GRAHAM

I haven't heard her throwing up in a while.

Phil and Graham listen.

PHIL

Maybe she's stopped.

Pause.

GRAHAM
(changing the subject)
So. How was the big first date?

PHIL

It was . . . good. It was really good. Until the end, of course.

GRAHAM

Of course. . . . She brought you home, huh?

PHIL
(waving him off in a get-outta-here way)
Stop it. . . .

GRAHAM

Well? She did!

PHIL

It's not like I haven't been here before. . . .

GRAHAM

So?! It's still a good sign!

PHIL

Yeah, maybe, but . . . I mean, we knew *you* were going to be here . . . although maybe we didn't know you were going to be quite so . . . *prominent*. . . .

GRAHAM

Yeah . . . I . . . I hope I didn't spoil the evening for you guys. . . .

PHIL

Oh . . . well . . . you know . . . I mean, you did. Without question, you did.

GRAHAM

Yeah. . . . Gee, you know, when I answered Tracy's roommate ad on craigslist, I never thought. . . . I mean, hey! My roommate and my oldest, bestest friend! I mean, who'd've thought?!

PHIL

Okay, well. It's still *new,* Graham. You know?

GRAHAM

Put in a good word for me, Phil.

PHIL

What?

GRAHAM

If she kicks me out of the apartment, I won't be able to stand it.

PHIL

She's not gonna kick you out. . . .

GRAHAM

She could, Phil. She could kick me out.

PHIL

She's a reasonable person; what happened was embarrassing, but she's not gonna overreact like that. . . .

GRAHAM

She's sensitive about . . . about this kind of stuff.

PHIL

You're freaking out over nothing. . . .

GRAHAM

I can't be rejected anymore, Phil. I can't stand it, I've been rejected so many times in my life. Put in a good word for me.

PHIL

I'll do what I can. Which is probably nothing.

Enter Tracy, with three empty glasses and a bottle of something. She doesn't look happy. She makes Phil and Graham nervous.

TRACY
(handing them glasses and pouring drinks for them)
I thought we could all use a drink.

PHIL

Good idea.

GRAHAM

Yeah, keep the party going, right? Woo! *(Graham's remark falls flat. Pause. Graham searches for some way to turn the tables.)* Listen, Tracy, I know you said you'd probably be out until midnight and I'd have the place to myself till then, but then you wound up coming home at half-past ten. And so you kind of, you know . . . surprised me. But I want you to know, I'm not pissed about you coming home early.

TRACY

You're not pissed off?

GRAHAM

Right. Even though you kind of surprised me.

TRACY

So you're not mad?

GRAHAM

Nah. These things happen.

TRACY

So you mean if you'd known when I was coming home you would have been masturbating to dirty movies in your room, instead of in the living room on my couch?

GRAHAM

Right. Or I would've masturbated earlier. *(Tracy gives him a look.)* But, I mean, probably in my room, yeah. And not on your couch.

TRACY

Why were you doing it in the living room, I wonder? On my couch?

GRAHAM

Well . . . like I said . . . I thought you'd be home at closer to midnight. . . .

TRACY

What I mean is, I didn't realize that any time I left the apartment you were whipping it out and rubbing yourself all over my thousand-dollar sofa that I like to curl up on after I've had a bath at night. I guess I always assumed you were doing that in your own room. Or at the very worst, in the shower. Which is why I always spray it down good before I step in.

GRAHAM

You don't have to worry about that, I always spray it down before I get out.

TRACY

Why were you masturbating in the living room on my couch, Graham?

GRAHAM

My laptop's busted.

TRACY

So?

GRAHAM

Well, the VCR's out here, and . . . I need a video. . . .

TRACY

Haven't you ever done it while just imagining a scenario in your *head?!*

GRAHAM
(smirking contemptuously)
Sure, when I was a *kid.*

PHIL

You should really train yourself to use your imagination, Graham. The things inside you, they're even better than a video.

TRACY

I'm sorry, Phil. When I invited you back here I had no idea that our date was going to end so grotesquely.

GRAHAM

I know Phil, *he* didn't mind!

PHIL

Actually Graham, I did mind some.

GRAHAM

Tracy, I *guarantee* you that Phil was not shocked.

PHIL

Okay, now. . . .

GRAHAM

Well were you?!

PHIL

I guess not, no. . . .

TRACY

All that proves is that he's a forgiving person.

GRAHAM

Hey, Phil has done stuff that makes what I just did look like . . . look like . . . well—anyway.

Pause.

TRACY

Phil. Have you ever masturbated in your roommate's living room—your *female* roommate's living room—even though you knew she might be coming home any minute?

PHIL

No.

TRACY

There. You see, Graham?

GRAHAM

You don't know the half of it. Tell her, Phil!

PHIL

Uh, maybe later, Graham! Like, someday.

GRAHAM

I mean, if you're liberal enough to go out with Phil here, I can't believe *anything* I do could shock you!

TRACY

Right. . . . Phil and I haven't really gotten to the point where we're exploring these, uh. . . .

GRAHAM

Tell her, Phil. . . .

PHIL

Uh, I don't know if. . . .

GRAHAM

Please tell her, I don't know what I'm gonna do if I have to move! . . .

PHIL

Well, maybe you could come stay with me! . . .

GRAHAM

I mean, Phil did it with his parents! . . .

PHIL and TRACY

Aa!

Phil's and Tracy's outbursts of pain cut Graham off, finally; Tracy claps her hands over her ears; Phil covers his face.

TRACY

I do not want to hear any more! *(Tracy looks up at Phil; she's suddenly tender as she thinks about his emotional needs.)* Until

. . . until Phil decides to tell me. If he does decide to tell me, that is. *(Phil uncovers his face and looks at Tracy with gratitude. Tracy turns back to Graham, harsh again.)* And as for you . . . I see just how much you can be trusted. Obviously Phil has taken you into his confidence about . . . certain things. Well, I know something about how painful disclosures like that can be. And I know something about the level of trust it takes to tell those things, to a friend. And that you would so cavalierly throw that trust away! . . . Well, just because Phil has evil, despicable parents. . . .

PHIL
Hey, now! . . . I mean . . . *evil.* . . .

TRACY
I know it's confusing . . . I know it can be hard to decide where your loyalties are. . . .

GRAHAM
He always said he liked it!

Tracy recoils.

PHIL
I said it was "rewarding."

TRACY
Okay, you know what, it's been an emotionally draining day, what with me getting psyched up for my big date, and you making love to yourself all over my couch, and you siding with your abusive parents. . . .

PHIL
My parents were not abusive. They were . . . free-thinking.

GRAHAM
Tell her, Phil!

PHIL
Well. Do you want to know?

Very long pause while Tracy decides.

92

TRACY

I think maybe I'd like to be done being grossed out today.

PHIL

Oh. Okay. So me, my family, and my childhood, we're all gross now.

TRACY

No, now I. . . .

PHIL

You know, you could have learned a lot from my parents.

TRACY

Oh, is that so?

PHIL

That is so. I like you, Tracy. You're smart. You're sexy. You're a good person. But you know what? You're also a little uptight. I always feel like I'm on the verge of offending you. If I make some little joke, or if I get a little too forward, or if there was some mild little kink in my upbringing. . . . I mean, after all, aren't we full-grown adults and not eleven-year-olds?

TRACY

And maybe I'd be different if I'd had your fabulous parents instead of my rotten ones.

PHIL

I'm not saying your parents were rotten. . . .

TRACY

I'm saying they were.

GRAHAM

Tell her what they did with you, Phil. Tell her where they took you. *(To Tracy:)* This is just beautiful. It makes me cry, for real.

TRACY

Fine. Tell me. Tell me about this amazing experience that I missed out on that would have made me a fuller, better person.

PHIL

Well. Okay. Fine. My parents. . . . *(Pause as Phil tries to think of how best to begin.)* You know I was raised in California.

TRACY

Yes.

PHIL

I grew up on this huge tract of land, far from any city. Perfect place to raise a boy. Even today I remember the satisfaction of getting our own food out of the earth, using the labor of our hands. . . .

TRACY

Your parents owned a farm?

PHIL

Well. More like a big garden. And there were other people there. And nobody really thought of themselves as *owning* anything.

TRACY

How many other people?

PHIL

It fluctuated. Sometimes dozens of people. Towards the end, not so many.

TRACY

A commune. You grew up on a commune.

Pause. Phil doesn't like to use the word "commune."

PHIL

I, yes, it was a commune. My parents were idealists.

GRAHAM

Tell her about the Masturbathon! *[pronounced MAS-tur-ba-thon]*

TRACY

The what?

94

PHIL

It was, like, a community event. It raised community spirit.

TRACY

It what? What was it?

GRAHAM

It was beautiful.

PHIL

It was kind of like a festival.

TRACY

It was a *what?* A Mass . . . something about masturbate?

PHIL

It was a festival, Tracy!

TRACY

A festival.

PHIL

You know how, in the olden days, like with hunter-gatherers, you would live with your tribe, and for most of your time you'd only see those couple dozen people. But then every once in a while there would be a festival, where a bunch of tribes got together and swapped stories, news, and ideas. That kind of thing.

TRACY

Wait, what's all this about hunter-gatherers? I thought you grew up on a *farm.*

PHIL

That's not really . . . uh . . . important. . . .

GRAHAM

Yeah, tell her about the *Masturbathon!!*

TRACY

This festival of yours was called the Masturbathon?

PHIL

It was a chance for people to get together and exchange
. . . ideas. . . . Several communities had—

TRACY

Communes.

PHIL

Right. Several *communes* had pitched in to buy a derelict
Gravitron from a down-on-its-luck carnival. You know the
Gravitron? It's a big wheel—a bunch of people are supposed
to stand inside it and it spins around and the centrifugal force
glues them against the wall and then it turns on its side and. . . .

TRACY

I know what a Gravitron is.

PHIL

Right. Well . . . ours was busted. It was just resting in an open
field. Once I turned eleven and hit puberty my parents decided
it was time for me to start attending the Masturbathon.

GRAHAM

God. That just sounds so *sane.* Do you know what *I* was doing
when I was eleven? Getting whipped by my father because he'd
caught me going through his stash of *Onion Booty Magazine.*

PHIL

I was a lucky boy.

TRACY

So you all went to this broken-down abandoned Gravitron out
in the middle of a field somewhere.

PHIL

Yes. We'd walk in, and those sheltering walls would enclose us,
and the blue sky would be overhead . . . and we'd stand in a big
circle, leaning against those old red carnie cushions, and. . . .
Gosh, you know, it was just a circle of love, you know, it really was.

GRAHAM

You must miss that so much. That freedom. That acceptance.

TRACY

Are you talking about a circle jerk?

PHIL

That's not what I would call it.

TRACY

You're talking about a circle jerk.

PHIL

I'm *talking* about a *Masturbathon.*

TRACY

What's the difference?

PHIL

That Masturbathon was . . . all right, I don't usually talk this way, but you want me to be honest? That Masturbathon was a beautiful circle of love and acceptance. Whereas a circle jerk comes from a place of shame.

GRAHAM

That's totally true. Believe me, I know.

TRACY

I'd agree that your little Masturbathon does indeed sound shame*less.*

PHIL

Okay, fine, yuk it up! I opened my heart to you but why should that mean anything. I mean, I bet there are goofy weird things that *your* family did that *I* could make fun of, if I wanted to. . . .

TRACY

We did some pretty hideous things. But, looking back, we did at least always have the decency to be ashamed of ourselves. I guess I can be proud of that, at least.

PHIL

Tracy, I hope this isn't going to be a big deal. . . .

TRACY

How often did this happen to you? Just the one time?

PHIL

Oh, no. The Masturbathon was held once or twice a month, and from the age of eleven I made it a point never to miss one, until I went away to college at eighteen. Not that there was much else to do out there in the middle of nowhere. You might say that I grew up at the Masturbathon.

TRACY

I'm looking at you and all I can see is hundreds of naked hippies beating off in a Gravitron.

PHIL

All right, hey, listen, Tracy—the truth is that . . . well, as I've made my way through the world, I've adapted. I've learned that something like the Masturbathon is . . . well, maybe a little too advanced for regular, everyday people. Spiritually advanced. But I've always searched for something that could take the place of that old childhood ritual. Something that could make me once more feel that sense of warmth, belonging, and acceptance. And when I'm with you—in those rare moments when you let your guard down—I almost feel like a relationship with you could be a path back to that place. That place of peace. Of joy.

TRACY

You're saying that being with me makes you feel like you and your parents and a bunch of hippies are jerking off in front of each other.

PHIL

Yes.

TRACY

In a broken-down old carnie ride.

PHIL

Yes. But you've got to remember, that was the best experience of my life. So it's a compliment.

TRACY

Well. I guess I feel like it only takes a minimal level of self-awareness to be embarrassed by having all your family and friends watch you masturbate.

PHIL
I see.

TRACY
I'm not trying to be cruel.

PHIL
Of course not.

TRACY
I just don't want to share my life with some cross between a human and a bonobo chimp.

PHIL
Gotcha.

TRACY
I'm not trying to be mean. It's not like what you're into *hurts* anyone. . . .

PHIL
That's all right. I guess you can't go back to Paradise, once you've been kicked out.

TRACY
Listen . . . you boys are fucked up. But that's okay! The world fucks everybody up. I'm fucked up, too. But our fucked-uppednesses . . . they aren't compatible. For example, I'm a little frigid. And I've always been afraid of intimacy because, well, frankly it's a little gross. As you have amply demonstrated.

PHIL
I wish I could bring you around. . . .

GRAHAM
Phil, man . . . you gotta pick your battles.

TRACY
It'll be okay. But we should go our separate ways. I'll probably

wind up marrying some tight-assed guy, the sort of man who screams in terror if your finger goes anywhere near his asshole. Early on in the relationship we'll choreograph one basic sexual routine, and we'll follow it until it becomes boring and, hence, non-threatening enough for the both of us to orgasm, more often than not.

PHIL
Whatever makes you happy.

TRACY
And meanwhile, you two boys will, you know, leave. I'm gonna go for a few drinks at a bar. Okay? And when I get back I would like it if neither of you were here.

GRAHAM
Please don't kick me out, Tracy! My internet will be back up soon!

TRACY
I'm sorry. It's just, you both seem kind of nasty to me now. Maybe I wouldn't mind getting a coffee sometime. But as far as living together, having sex with each other, all that—not happening, sorry. *(Tracy's about to leave; she notices how dejected Phil looks, and stops.)* Aw, Phil, don't take it so hard. We only ever even went out on one date.

PHIL
Ah, never mind me, I'm just being stupid. . . .

TRACY
Jesus, Phil. Are you crying?

PHIL
I know this won't make any sense, logically. But there was this one old guy from the next commune over. Ernie. Ernie was kind of a broken-down old man. Prematurely aged. Long, tangled gray hair. A big bushy beard. He had a nervous air. The muscles around his eyes were always bunched up. You could tell that life had put him through the wringer, and he didn't want to get burned again. Sort of like you. Anyway,

100

I remember the way Ernie was when he'd let his guard down, in that Gravitron, during the Masturbathon. Those little muscles around his eyes would loosen and those eyes would just *dance*. And, well . . . I guess it sounds crazy, but that was how I wanted to make *you* feel, Tracy.

Pause.

TRACY

Bye.

Exit Tracy.

Pause.

GRAHAM

You want to talk about it?

PHIL

Nah. I'm going to give her enough time to get out of the building and out of sight . . . get a block or two away . . . and then I'm just going to head home.

GRAHAM

Don't you want to talk about it?

PHIL

No, actually, I don't, Graham. I really just would like to be alone right now.

Pause.

GRAHAM

You know, the reason why I need the videos . . . really, it's for the company. I just don't like to be alone. . . . I'm feeling lonely, but then when I put the video on, I'm with people all of a sudden. . . .

PHIL

What are you saying, Graham?

GRAHAM

You told Tracy that you wanted to see the kind of change in her that you used to see in Hippie Ernie. Well, Tracy's gone, but maybe I can be your Ernie. And maybe you can be mine.

Graham tentatively puts his hands on his fly.

PHIL

Graham, hey—I know what you're thinking, but this— *(Phil gestures at the room as a whole.)* —this is no Masturbathon.

GRAHAM

Phil. It's not how many people there are, that makes it a Masturbathon. It's not whether it's in a Gravitron or not. It's about the heart. *(Pause.)* And other organs.

They both laugh.

PHIL

All right, what the hell.

GRAHAM

Really?! You'll do it with me?!

PHIL

Yeah, I got no place special to be.

GRAHAM

Oh, you've made me so happy! That's all I've ever wanted, was not to be alone while I did it.

PHIL

I know, Graham.

GRAHAM

Oh, Phil. It doesn't get any better than this.

PHIL

I'm afraid that's so.

BLACKOUT

LOVE STINKS

CHARACTERS:

Brian
Fiona
Maggie

We're in Fiona's farmhouse, cluttered with exotic curios and bric-a-brac, but the dialogue should be enough to suggest all that—all we really need are three chairs, or two should be fine if Brian never sits down. That having been said, Fiona does have to pick up a glass vial (like, an empty perfume bottle or something) and hand it to Maggie, and she has to pick it up from somewhere, so maybe there could just be a few bottles or vials or whatever laid out on a rehearsal cube to signify the plethora we're being asked to see in our mind's eye. We're also gonna need a box that looks like doughnuts came in it. We won't need any doughnuts.

Lights up. Maggie and Fiona are seated, paying more attention to each other than to Brian. They're ill at ease around each other. Brian is excited, and doesn't notice.

BRIAN

It's so great to be seeing you again, Fiona!

FIONA

It's great to see you, too, Brian.

BRIAN

And to be back in your house and everything. I always did think you had just the neatest place—all these antiques and curios and exotic doodads and dusty bottles full of herbs and potions and stuff. . . .

FIONA

Can't cram *all* my wares into the shop.

MAGGIE

How is the old shop? Old "Mme Fiona's Curios, Magic, Psychic Readings, etc., etc."?

FIONA

Same as ever. You know how it is. Not a huge number of customers. But I've got a select, loyal clientele that spends enough to keep me in this dump, at least.

BRIAN

I love this old farmhouse!

FIONA

"Old" is right. And drafty.

BRIAN

But it's got character! And it's great how isolated it is. You could throw a huge party and never get any noise complaints.

FIONA

Probably. I don't really throw parties. I'm alone, mostly.

BRIAN

Really, it is just great to see you. I'm always saying to Maggie, "Hey, how come we never see Fiona anymore? Didn't we all used to be practically best friends?" I don't think Maggie and I have seen you at all since we started dating!

FIONA

No. I don't guess you have.

MAGGIE

I don't guess we have. *(Pause.)* Hey, Brian. You know what I would like?

BRIAN

Whatever it is, if it's something I can get then you'll have it soon, angel. Do you want a diamond? Do you want a rose? Do you want the moon?! Do you want the sun?! Do you—

MAGGIE

I'd like some doughnuts.

BRIAN

You want some doughnuts?

MAGGIE

I would, yes.

BRIAN

You got 'em.

MAGGIE

Awesome. I remember we passed a doughnut shop right before we turned off the main road. Do you remember?

BRIAN

It was part of a gas station.

MAGGIE

Yeah, exactly. Could you be a good boy and go get us a box?

BRIAN

Uh, sure, I. . . .You know what? On second thought, I'm not quite a hundred, hundred percent sure I remember where it is. Maybe you could come with me? . . .

MAGGIE

I'd sort of like to talk to Fiona for a while, hon. Like you said, we haven't seen her in a long time.

BRIAN

We could *all* go! . . .

MAGGIE

Brian. Remember what we talked about the other day?

BRIAN

Um. . . .

MAGGIE

About how we can't be together every single second of every day? And we need at least a little time apart, at least every once in a while?

BRIAN

Yes.

MAGGIE

And you said you'd agree, if that was what I wanted? And I said that I did want it?

BRIAN

Yes.

MAGGIE

Well. Then why does it suddenly feel like that whole conversation never happened?

BRIAN

Yes, uh, but, well, see, the thing is . . . that doughnut shop is probably a ten-minute drive there and back, and, well. . . .

MAGGIE

Yes?

BRIAN

Well, you didn't mean for us to be apart *that* long, did you?

MAGGIE

Brian!

BRIAN

Okay, okay, I'm going! I'm going. Any doughnut flavor requests? Fiona?

FIONA

Well. . . .

MAGGIE

Just get an assortment, Brian.

BRIAN

An assortment. Okay, sure thing. So, uh . . . well . . . well, bye, Maggie, honey, bye.

MAGGIE

Bye.

BRIAN

Yeah. Goodbye. Bye, baby.

MAGGIE

Bye, Brian. I'll see you again extremely soon.

BRIAN

Okay. Well. I'm off. I'm. . . . Bye, honey—

MAGGIE

Bye, Brian!

BRIAN

Okay! Okay . . . bye. . . .

Brian forces himself to exit. Fiona and Maggie look at each other a moment before speaking.

FIONA

That sort of looked like you were getting rid of him so that we could speak alone.

MAGGIE

I guess that is sort of what it was.

FIONA

Okay. Well.

MAGGIE

Well.

FIONA

Well.

MAGGIE

Well. He'll be back in a minute.

FIONA

Yes. So I guess you've only got a little while to tell me . . . whatever it is you're wanting to tell me.

MAGGIE

I think you know what I'm wanting to tell you.

FIONA

No.

MAGGIE

Come on. You can guess.

FIONA

No. No clue. *(Pause.)* Are . . . are things between you and Brian
. . . are they? . . .

MAGGIE

Are they all right?

FIONA

Right. Nothing . . . wrong?

MAGGIE

He does everything I always hoped a man would do.

FIONA

Aw.

MAGGIE

He's always there. He's completely supportive.

FIONA

That's wonderful.

MAGGIE

He even managed to arrange it so that he works from home
now. It wasn't easy, getting his boss to agree. I think if his boss
hadn't agreed, he would have quit his job.

FIONA

He sure is devoted.

MAGGIE

Yeah. It's been a big adjustment for me. Because, you know,
I work from home too. So I was used to having a bunch of alone
time. But now, what with him having moved in, and not going
to the office anymore, we're together an awful lot. Pretty much
all the time.

FIONA

What a rare, beautiful chance to build up a real intimacy. You know, most couples never get that chance.

MAGGIE

Meanwhile, God forbid anyone should ever say the slightest thing bad about me. One of my editors sent me a perfectly polite e-mail about some revisions he wanted me to do on a piece. And Brian nearly called him up and challenged him to a duel.

FIONA

He's chivalrous on top of everything else. They don't make them like that anymore.

MAGGIE

I had to physically pull him away from the phone.

FIONA

He's a passionate man.

MAGGIE

I feel like you must be able to tell from my expression and my tone of voice that I'm, uh, ambivalent about all this.

FIONA

I was hoping for the best.

MAGGIE

Yeah. Well.

FIONA

Relationships can be tough. Sometimes two people have to put in a lot of effort if they want them to work.

MAGGIE

Fuck that, I want it to *stop* working! And it's not just two people, it's three! You're involved in this, too! He's choking me! He's like if there were a huge extremely dense clot of hair shoved down into a garbage disposal and you couldn't run it anymore. That's what my life is like now!

FIONA

Okay, hey, look—I may be *involved*. But I'm not *responsible*.

MAGGIE

Okay. I freaked out. Sorry. But still—you have to admit, none of this would have ever happened if it hadn't been for you.

FIONA

Jesus. Listen to yourself. Yeah, that's right—none of it ever would have happened if not for me. And why did I do it? Because a year ago a certain someone came to me in tears, begging me, even though she knew how I felt about . . . well . . . never mind.

MAGGIE

I'm sorry. I'm just, I'm going crazy.

FIONA

Well try to have a little consideration for me.

MAGGIE

Okay. I will. But . . . you must be able to do something!

FIONA

And what if I can't? You remember how you came to me and begged me to sell you a love potion? And how I said, "Careful, now. You don't want to screw around with this stuff—once it takes, it sticks." And you said you were certain.

MAGGIE

I was. Then.

FIONA

Of course, I didn't realize you wanted a love potion so you could give it to the man I was in love with.

MAGGIE

Infatuated with.

FIONA

In love with.

MAGGIE

Infatuated with.

FIONA

You're pissing me off.

MAGGIE

Okay, look—I miscalculated, all right? I misjudged the depths of your feelings for Brian. And I misjudged the, you know, the shallowness of mine. But now I'm asking you to help me put things right. Partly for my sake—we've known each other such a long time, Fiona. But also for Brian's sake. Because he deserves better than to be slavishly devoted for all eternity to someone who wishes he would just get lost. And also, you know . . . for your sake. Because maybe, if you really do feel that way about him, you might still have a chance to make it work. If only he weren't magically bonded to me to the point where he can't look at another woman.

FIONA

How altruistic of you.

MAGGIE

I was wrong, okay? Brian is not "the one" for me. And I want to be able to, you know, try again with someone else. Date other people.

FIONA

And what if the spell is irreversible? What if, once he drank the love potion, that was it? No turning back?

MAGGIE

Then, god damn it, I'll make him so miserable that he'll either finally leave me alone, or else he'll be curled up in a ball on the floor and I won't have to worry about him anymore. . . . Or no, you know what I'll do? I'll tell him, "If you really loved me, you'd blow your brains out."

FIONA

You couldn't do that!

MAGGIE

I could!

FIONA

It wouldn't work. He'd never do it.

MAGGIE

Oh, he would do *anything* I told him to. Believe me. It's disgusting.

FIONA

He loves you. He's deeply in love with you.

MAGGIE

Well, *fix* that! Or else!

Pause.

FIONA

Okay. Okay. There might be a way.

MAGGIE

Good.

FIONA

But there could be side effects.

MAGGIE

Keep going.

FIONA

Well. The way the love potion works is that, last year, when you slipped it into Brian's beer, as soon as he drank it, his pheromones became perfectly interfaced with yours.

MAGGIE

Duh, I know all that.

Fiona goes to get a little vial, which she then gives to Maggie.

FIONA

The trick now is that we have to adjust your chemical balance so that the pheromones no longer match up. Brian will find his interest fading and, since you won't be trying to rekindle it, things'll naturally come to an end.

MAGGIE

And that little vial will do that?

FIONA

This little vial should do that.

MAGGIE

And, uh—side effects?

FIONA

Pretty minor. See, when you readjust your chemistry like that, what happens is. . . . Did you ever go on the Atkins Diet?

MAGGIE

Ugh, Jesus. I was exhausted the whole time, and it made my armpits smell like rotting meat.

FIONA

Exactly—the Atkins Diet corpse smell. Well, something similar happens with this.

MAGGIE

Aw, jeez. I don't know.

FIONA

You gotta be kidding me. A minute ago you were willing to kill an innocent man who loves you!

MAGGIE

But that was such a bad smell.

FIONA

Look, this is not an easy potion to reverse! You have to be willing to make an effort!

MAGGIE

Okay, okay. . . . It wears off, right? The smell?

FIONA

Oh, sure, sure. . . .

MAGGIE

Okay, well . . . let's do it. . . .

FIONA

Bottoms up.

Maggie drinks the vial. Pause.

MAGGIE

I don't feel any different.

FIONA

You probably won't be able to notice anything. Except for the, uh, side effect I mentioned.

From here, both women gradually become aware of an intensifying stench, which they try to refrain from mentioning, until Maggie's outburst.

MAGGIE

Okay. . . . Hey, Fiona—thank you.

FIONA

Yeah. No problem.

MAGGIE

You're a real friend. And I know I haven't always been a good one. Like when I kind of sort of nabbed Brian out from under you.

FIONA

You mean like when you kind of sort of tricked me into selling you a magic love potion without telling me you were going to use it on the man I loved?

MAGGIE

Yeah. I guess so. . . . Fiona, can I ask you something?

FIONA

Sure, why not.

MAGGIE

I've always wondered . . . if you were so into Brian, why didn't you ever slip him the love potion yourself?

FIONA

Don't think I wasn't tempted. I mean, obviously I don't have some big moral objection to all these charms and spells and stuff, or I wouldn't sell them. But with Brian . . . I don't know. I guess I always had the fantasy that he would maybe one day want me just for me, you know? For my own sake.

MAGGIE

Huh. . . . Well, maybe now you'll get your chance.

FIONA

Oh. I don't know. In my experience, it's not so easy to go back in time. To fix things. To grab opportunities that you missed the first time around.

MAGGIE

Yeah, well, I, uh . . . Jesus, I can barely breathe!

FIONA

Yeah, that's pretty extreme.

MAGGIE

Is that smell coming from me?! From my body?!

FIONA

Afraid so.

MAGGIE

So I can't get away from it?!

FIONA

Don't see how.

MAGGIE

Jesus! How am I going to survive?!

FIONA

Uh. People adapt to all sorts of stuff, I guess.

MAGGIE

It's only a temporary side effect, right? How long does it last?

Enter Brian.

BRIAN

Hey, I found some chocolate-filled . . . oh, God.

FIONA

Breathe through your mouth, Brian. It makes it a little easier.

BRIAN

What are you guys just hanging around for?! Are you crazy?! We've gotta get outta here!

FIONA

Brian. Maggie *can't* get away from that smell.

BRIAN

Wha. . . . You mean? . . .

MAGGIE

Afraid so, hon.

BRIAN

Did you eat some really old beans or something?

MAGGIE

No.

BRIAN

Oh, sweetie, come on, let's take you to the bathroom and get you cleaned up. . . .

MAGGIE

What?! No! God!

BRIAN

But baby, you don't have to be embarrassed in front of me, not about anything. I love you. Completely. Unconditionally.

MAGGIE

Fiona!

FIONA

I could die happy if someone said that to me just once, and meant it.

BRIAN

Aw, Fiona—you're a beautiful person, you'll find that special someone someday . . . but for right now . . . for right now we've got to do something about my baby!

MAGGIE

Don't you feel any different about me, Brian?!

BRIAN

What? Of course not!

MAGGIE

Are you sure?! Because you don't have to feel obligated to stay with me if your feelings have changed! Even if they only just changed a minute ago! We're both free adults!

BRIAN

Maggie—I love you. My feelings for you are . . . well, they're almost magical! And they will never change, no matter what. Never, ever, ever.

MAGGIE

Fiona. . . .

FIONA

Most women would feel pretty lucky to hear a man say something like that. Especially, well, not to be rude, but especially if they smelled the way you smell.

Pause.

MAGGIE

Fiona. How long am I going to smell this way?

FIONA

Well, um . . . forever?

BRIAN and MAGGIE

Forever?!

FIONA

Or, well, until you die, I mean. After you die I guess you'll probably smell a little bit better.

MAGGIE

That's your "temporary side effect"? So when you say "temporary," you mean "temporary" as in, "life is temporary," "the universe is temporary"?

BRIAN

Uh. . . . Side effect? . . .

FIONA

I guess, Maggie, the truth is I kind of tricked you. For better or for worse Brian is stuck being in love with you for the rest of his life. If you leave him he'll just pine away till he dies. I couldn't let you ruin his life by dumping him and sneaking off to where he couldn't find you. And I *certainly* couldn't let you make him kill himself.

BRIAN

Kill myself?!

MAGGIE

Did I take an antidote to that love potion, or not?!

BRIAN

Love potion? . . . What? . . . Hey—hey, you listen here, Fiona. There's no "love potion" involved here. I love Maggie from the heart—pure and simple—why, I'll never forget the moment I realized what an amazingly special lady she is. We were having a drink in a bar. I was looking away from her, at the game on the TV. It's amazing to me now, that I was able to pay attention to some dumb football game when I had this miraculous creature right there next to me, that I didn't even appreciate yet! But then I looked away from the TV, and took a sip of my beer, and then looked back over at Maggie. And as soon as I looked at her it just hit me what an exquisite and beautiful and perfect and—

MAGGIE

Can it, Brian!

FIONA

I think you ought to be nice to him. Because you like men. And he loves you. And I don't think you're going to find any more men besides him who are going to be willing to touch you. Or even be in the same room with you for very long.

MAGGIE

You mean. . . .

FIONA

Yeah. I hit you with a stinky spell.

MAGGIE

You . . . *bitch.*

BRIAN

Hey . . . come on, guys. . . .

FIONA

But you know something, Maggie? I would still trade places with you in a second. Because you get to have this guy here. The man of my dreams.

BRIAN

What? What are you saying, Fiona? . . . You guys, I'm very confused.

FIONA

Maybe now you'll finally learn some appreciation, Maggie.

MAGGIE

Yeah. Maybe. But first maybe I'll teach *you* something. Grab her, Brian!

BRIAN

But . . . honey. . . .

MAGGIE

What did I tell you before about not doing what I say, Brian?!

BRIAN

You . . . uh . . . you. . . .

MAGGIE

What did I tell you would happen to you if you didn't mind me?!

BRIAN

You told me you would make me take off all my clothes, and write "I do not deserve my girlfriend's love" on my naked body, and walk around the street that way until the police arrested me, and then they would take me to jail, and you would never come and visit me. And that I would probably get too depressed to eat, and probably starve and die.

MAGGIE

That's right. And that's just the beginning of what's going to happen to you if Fiona leaves this room.

Fiona makes a break for it; Brian grabs her, holds her from behind by the arms, so that she's facing Maggie.

BRIAN

Gee, sorry about this, Fiona.

FIONA

That's okay, Brian. This is all more my fault than yours, if you only knew.

MAGGIE

So how do I get this smell to go away, Fiona?

FIONA

I already told you. You'll have to drop dead.

MAGGIE

You better start talking really fucking fast.

FIONA

Sorry. It's like the potion. No antidote.

MAGGIE

Huh. Okay. Well what do you think we should do about this, then?

FIONA

Um. Let bygones be bygones? Call ourselves even and go our separate ways?

MAGGIE

I'm not sure I'd call this "even." *(Maggie sniffs her own armpit, gags.)* This almost feels like a violent-revenge sort of situation. You know?

FIONA

I guess I knew when I gave you that vial that that was a possible outcome.

MAGGIE

Yeah, well, glad you're prepared. Hey, Brian, honey, grab something sharp and slit her throat.

BRIAN

No!

MAGGIE

Brian, honey, what was I just telling you a second ago was going to happen if you didn't do what I say?!

BRIAN

I don't care! I can't kill somebody, and especially not Fiona! She's my friend, and it's wrong.

MAGGIE

You're going to make me so mad that I'm going to go away and you'll never be able to find me.

FIONA

You could probably track her by scent.

BRIAN

Please. Please, baby. I'm really begging you. Ask me to do anything but that, and I'll do it.

MAGGIE

All right. You can kill Fiona, or you can kill yourself.

BRIAN

I. . . . I. . . . Okay. I'd rather do that, then. I'd rather do it to myself.

FIONA

Brian!

MAGGIE

Shit. . . . All right. Fine. You kill her, or I'll kill myself.

BRIAN

You wouldn't!

MAGGIE

The world isn't big enough to hold both me and the woman who made me smell this way.

BRIAN

I. . . . Hey, Fiona . . . I can't take that chance. . . .

FIONA

I know you can't, sweetie.

BRIAN

Gee, I'm sorry. . . .

FIONA

Don't worry. If there's anyone who understands, it's me.

MAGGIE

Get it over with so we can get the fuck out of here.

BRIAN

I. . . . Maggie, would you really commit suicide?

MAGGIE

Smelling like this?! Forever?! I might off myself any second now.

FIONA

Pee-yew! No one would blame you!

MAGGIE

Go on, hurry. I saw some razors in the bathroom. Go kill her in there so she's easier to clean up after.

Brian starts dragging Fiona backstage.

FIONA

Nice knowing you, Maggie! Glad I had a chance to let you know how I really feel about you!

Exit Brian and Fiona.

Maggie walks center-stage, stands looking out at the audience. She raises her arm and smells her own armpit again.

MAGGIE

Gah! That is fucking unbearable!

Pause. Maggie sniffs her armpit again, and considers the smell; it still stinks, but she's able to be a little more philosophical about it now.

MAGGIE

Meh. You can get used to anything, I guess.

Fiona screams off-stage. The scream is abruptly cut off. Maggie doesn't even seem to notice it.

Cue music.

BLACKOUT

PART III

SOMEONE BORROWED, SOMEONE SCREWED

CHARACTERS:

Beth: 20's or 30's. Kristy's fiancée.
Kristy: 20's or 30's. Beth's fiancée.
Steven: 20's or 30's. Kristy's brother.

SETTING:

Astoria, Queens.

The lights go up on Beth and Steven staring at each other, frozen in shock. Beth is shocked and horrified, whereas Steven is only shocked.

BETH
Okay, so, uh . . . she's going to be back any minute, so, uh. . . .

STEVEN
I still, so, uh . . . *Beth?!*

BETH
You're her brother?! . . . Steven? You're *that* Steven? . . . *(Hopefully)* Or, maybe, no! Maybe you're here for some totally different reason?! . . .

STEVEN
I'm . . . here for my sister's wedding.

BETH

Dammit.

STEVEN

To a woman named Beth.

BETH

Dammit.

STEVEN

Who I guess is you.

BETH

Obviously it's me!

STEVEN

Well I wasn't expecting you to be *that* Beth! I thought you'd be some other Beth!

BETH

Obviously you did! And you were right to expect that, because this is totally insane! . . . Jesus. What're we gonna do. . . . She's out. She went to grab some groceries. She's out now but she'll probably be back soon, because she felt guilty about leaving in the first place, about not meeting you at the airport.

STEVEN

I didn't want to put you guys to any trouble. And I liked making my way here from the airport. It was sort of an adventure.

BETH

Uh-huh. I want to do the right thing here. I want to figure out the right thing. So, we have to . . . God. It's you. What are we gonna tell her?

STEVEN

Beth.

BETH

Yeah?

STEVEN

It's good to see you again, Beth.

Pause.

BETH

What?

STEVEN

I said it's good to see you again. And it's a big surprise.

BETH

It sure is!

STEVEN

I always figured we'd meet again someday.

BETH

You did?

STEVEN

Yeah. Fate.

BETH

Kristy's going to be back soon. My fiancée, your sister. . . .
Right? She really is your sister? You really are *that* Steven?

STEVEN

She's my step-sister. And you really are that Beth.

BETH

I just, I can't believe this is happening. . . .

STEVEN

Beth. Don't I get a hug?

BETH

What?

STEVEN

I haven't seen you in years.

BETH

Oh.

Beth hugs him perfunctorily, tries to draw away; he holds her back, albeit not in a creepily forceful way.

STEVEN

Beth, hey, listen, I . . . I mean, let's at least take a few minutes to soak this up, right?! I got on a plane in Dallas to come to my sister's wedding in New York. And you answer the door. It's a miracle!

BETH

(pulling away)

That's one word for it. Listen, Kristy will be home soon and, uh. . . . She's a little high-strung.

STEVEN

No shit, you don't have to tell me that. I've known her since our parents got married when she was ten.

BETH

What I mean is, she's *especially* high-strung. At the moment. What with the wedding, and what with nobody from our families coming. Except you, and her two cousins in Philly. So . . . so I think it would be for the best if we didn't, ah . . . like, maybe she doesn't need to know that we know each other. . . .

STEVEN

What?!

BETH

Well?! I guess it's a little dishonest, but it's . . . isn't it for the best, don't you think?

STEVEN

No.

BETH

It would come out, wouldn't it?

STEVEN

I don't want to keep all that a secret.

BETH

Okay. Okay. You're right, it's too big, I don't know if I can stand lying to her *that* much . . . but she doesn't need to know about *us,* us. Like, she can know that we know each other. But she doesn't have to know that we have a past and all.

STEVEN

If we don't have a past then how do we know each other?

BETH

Just, maybe we know each other from around.

STEVEN

Around?

BETH

Yeah, you know. Like, around town. Around Dallas. Friends of friends. That kind of thing.

STEVEN

You mean like we were casual acquaintances.

BETH

Yes. The kind of thing that we can talk about for a while without it seeming weird.

STEVEN

That kind of hurts my feelings, Beth.

BETH

I'm sorry. I just am not sure what to do. But Kristy is about to be my wife, and I don't want her to find out that. . . . I especially don't want her to be thinking about that, just now. Don't take it personally.

STEVEN

How am I supposed to not take it personally? It's a very personal thing.

BETH

Just, please, Steven. For old times' sake!

                    STEVEN
                   (reluctantly)
Since it's you asking.

                     BETH
Sh, I hear her coming in. . . .

Enter Kristy, with grocery bags.

                    KRISTY
Well, hey there!

                    STEVEN
Hey yourself!

                     BETH
Look, Kristy, your step-brother's here!

                    KRISTY
You guys met already?

                    STEVEN
We sure did.

                     BETH
Yeah, that's right! And in fact, Kristy, it's, uh, kinda crazy, but
. . . we know each other!

                    KRISTY
What?! From Texas?!

                     BETH
That's right!

                    KRISTY
How?!

                     BETH
Oh, just, like . . . from a bar. . . .

                    KRISTY
From a bar?

BETH

Well, there were other people around. . . .

STEVEN

Usually is, in a bar.

KRISTY

So . . . friends of friends?

BETH

Um. Sure.

KRISTY

That is amazing.

BETH

It's funny. It's pretty crazy.

KRISTY

Well. . . . Wow. . . . We *all* have some catching up to do!

STEVEN

That's right.

KRISTY

So . . . but I guess you guys didn't keep in touch, right? Because that would be too nuts, if you knew she'd moved to New York and was going to marry a woman, and also knew that I was going to marry a woman named Beth, and you still hadn't worked it out. . . .

STEVEN

That would have been nuts, yeah.

BETH

We were only really hanging out for seven or eight weeks.

KRISTY

Oh. That's specific. You make it sound like you were at camp or something.

BETH

No, we just did . . . normal stuff. . . .

STEVEN
Yeah. Movies. Dinners.

KRISTY
When was all this?

BETH
Oh. Three years ago, I guess. Maybe a year and a half before I moved to New York.

STEVEN
Yeah. It was May and June of 2007.

BETH
Or sometime around then.

STEVEN
It was right when the Spurs beat the Cavs for the NBA Championships.

KRISTY
Wow. . . . It sounds like you guys, uh, hung out a lot.

Pause.

STEVEN
Hey, Beth, listen. This is crazy.

BETH
Uh, what is, Steven?!

STEVEN
Let's just tell her.

KRISTY
Tell me?

Pause. Steven keeps looking at Beth.

BETH
Kristy, the weird thing is that Steven and I didn't just "know" each other. We actually dated for a while.

KRISTY

Oh. . . . For seven or eight weeks, I gather. In May and June of 2007.

STEVEN

It was actually like seven and a half weeks. We met on a Saturday. And we saw each other for the last time on like a Wednesday.

KRISTY

Wow.

BETH

Isn't that so freaky, hon?

KRISTY

It sure is. *(Pause.)* I mean what the fuck?!

STEVEN

Whoa, Kristy! It's just, like, a six-degrees thing!

KRISTY

So you guys, what, you fucking dated each other?!

BETH

Well. Yes. Briefly.

KRISTY

All right, I, hey . . . you know what? I need to be alone for a minute.

BETH

Kristy, baby, come on. . . .

STEVEN

Just let her go, Beth. . . .

BETH

Uh, could you stay out of this?!

KRISTY

Excuse me.

Exit Kristy.

STEVEN

Don't worry. She'll be fine.

BETH

No thanks to you. Why did you tell her that? I thought we agreed that we were just going to act like we'd known each other but not dated. Now you've made us look awful.

Beth doesn't really pay attention to Steven during the following bit; her mind is on Kristy.

STEVEN

I know. But we started talking and I realized that I just wasn't going to be able to go through with it. I don't want to lie and pretend that time never happened because, I mean . . . it was important to me. It didn't last very long, but it was important to me, and it's something I think about pretty often. And to have to pretend that none of it ever happened, for the rest of my life . . . well, I just couldn't stand that. You hear what I'm saying, Beth?

BETH

What? . . . Oh. Yeah. Uh, I understand, Steven, sure, but. . . .

STEVEN

This might sound . . . well . . . the truth is, I always have an eye out for you. When I pop in to a bar, when I'm at the mall. Even when I'm with other women. But here in New York . . . it's like the universe waited until the exact moment that it knew I wouldn't be expecting you.

BETH

Yeah. That's sweet, Steven. But maybe we should talk about it later. . . .

STEVEN

I mean, I'm standing here and telling you that I *looked* for you, Beth. I *looked* for you. And even a year and a half after the last time I saw you, I every once in a while would call up your number and hope you'd answer. And then when you didn't I'd leave a message, and hope you'd call back, even though you never did. So, you can see, meeting you here, that means something to me.

BETH

Steven. I know that you used to call, and leave messages, and that I never called you back.

STEVEN

Oh . . . right. I get it. . . .

BETH

Yeah. Listen, I'm going to go and try to talk to her.

STEVEN

All right.

BETH

Just, I don't know. Make yourself at home, okay? We have, like, books and stuff that you could look at.

STEVEN

Sure. Or I have my own books. In my bag, I packed some.

BETH

Okay. . . . Well. I'll be back.

Beth crosses to the side of the stage where Kristy is sitting and staring ahead of herself. Lights dim on Steven. Our attention isn't directed towards him, but when we do look at him we see that he isn't, say, slumped over or staring idly into space; he looks excited, like he's thinking about or planning something. Beth walks softly up to Kristy.

BETH
(soothingly)
Hey, sweetie. Things are going to be all right. Aren't they?

Pause.

KRISTY

This feels like a deal-breaker.

137

BETH

What?

KRISTY

I mean, things were not exactly not-tense already. With my family. What with no one coming for my wedding. Except for my cousins Maria and Danny. And Steven.

BETH

How dare you say that to me? Who cares whether or not your family takes us seriously? I thought we were really going to do this. Really be a couple for life, and fuck what everybody thinks. Our families, the government, everybody. . . . And besides, people are coming to our wedding. We have fifty guests RSVPed for our wedding. Who cares if our stupid *families* doesn't show up? *My* family's not coming. Do you see that bothering *me?*

KRISTY

It's *getting* to me. I can't help it. I thought I'd be able to deal, but they're *getting* to me. My family. They never had a problem with me being gay—not *too* big a problem—but the wedding . . . they act like it's this big joke that's too sophisticated for them, that goes right over their heads. . . . "But that's not *legal* yet, is it? Not even in New York." "No, Mom. It won't be a *legal* wedding. But we're going to have the ceremony. So we'll be married in a, whatever, in a spiritual sense." "Oh. That's nice, dear."

BETH

They don't get it. It's a weird idea for them. Give them time.

KRISTY

"Mom, do you think maybe you might be able to fly up? For my wedding?" "Well, honey, I have some vacation time due a couple months later, we'll probably just come up then."

BETH

Okay, I feel like you're mad because I used to know your brother—

KRISTY

Used to *carnally* know him.

BETH

Fine. Used to *date* him. . . . You're mad about that, and you're also mad because your parents aren't taking our relationship very seriously. You're mad about both those things at the same time, and those two angers are sort of feeding off each other, and you're getting madder and madder. But you're losing sight of the fact that those two things, they don't actually have anything to do with each other, except that they're in the same place at the same moment. So try to calm down, and, if you want to get mad about this stuff, please get mad about it one thing at a time. . . .

KRISTY

These two things have to do with one another. Because this thing with you and my brother . . . it makes us look like a joke. And I can't handle being a joke. Like, some clown, whose siblings aren't real siblings, whose parents aren't real parents, whose spouse isn't a real spouse. . . .

BETH

Baby . . . it'll be all right, after a while. . . .

KRISTY

And then Steven. . . . I mean, you know what it is? . . . Or no, I shouldn't even tell you, you'll be offended.

BETH

Now you have to tell me.

Pause.

KRISTY

He used to steal my toys. Or "borrow" them. He called it "borrowing" them. And he'd always . . . get them dirty. Leave sticky fingerprints on them. Mark them in some way. Or leave them in his room. He wouldn't put them back in mine, he'd leave them in his room, so it'd be like, Well, if they're all marked up from his having handled them, and if they're in his room and not mine, what makes them mine instead of his? . . . I am so ashamed right now, telling you this. I mean, how ridiculous is it that this shit should have any bearing on our lives as adults?

BETH

You carry stuff with you.

Enter Steven, knocking on the doorframe.

STEVEN

Hey. Knock, knock. Can I, uh. . . . Everything okay?

KRISTY

Jesus, Steven. Can you not ever learn to knock?

STEVEN

I did. Like this.

Steven knocks on the frame again.

KRISTY

Stop being an asshole. You've been barging into my rooms since I was a kid and you only do it to make me crazy.

STEVEN

I'm sorry. I guess I was thinking of it as a gag, to sort of break the tension . . . and sort of as a reminder of, you know, when we were kids. . . . Never mind, that's stupid. . . . I hope I didn't. . . . I hope I wasn't. . . . Hi, Beth. . . . Sorry, I'll shut up. . . .

Steven retreats from the doorway and out of the room, back to his own side of the stage.

KRISTY

I was bitchy, wasn't I.

BETH

Well. He should have knocked.

KRISTY

But he flew all the way up here. He spent money on a ticket to come and show his support to me, when no one else in the family did. So I owe him. . . . Jesus. Did you ever tell me about him? As one of the guys you dated?

BETH

Oh, probably in passing. . . .

KRISTY

Was whatever you said complimentary?

BETH

Ummm. . . .

KRISTY

Never mind never mind never mind, I don't want to know. It's not like any of the guys you ever told me about sounded like prizes. Like that one you told me about, who—

BETH

Let's not get distracted, talking about all that.

KRISTY

All right.

BETH

I've dated guys. That never seemed like a huge problem before.

KRISTY

Guys. Yes. Anonymous, faceless guys. Random penises. Kinky footnotes in your sexual history. You see where I'm going with this?

BETH

You never imagined one of those faceless multitudes as being your brother.

KRISTY

Riiiiiiiiight. . . . I also never really imagined them as "multitudes," either, so thanks for that.

BETH

Are you mad at me?

KRISTY

Yup.

BETH

But. Honey, it's not my fault. When I was with Steven, I had no idea yet that you even existed. And then once you and I started going out . . . how was I supposed to know that this woman I started going out with in New York had a brother that I'd had a thing with in Texas?

KRISTY

On the one hand there's that. The fact that none of this is your fault and you couldn't have known. Then on the other hand there's the fact that you fucked my brother.

BETH

Don't say it like that.

KRISTY

Was it a really casual thing, at least?

BETH

Well. . . .

KRISTY

It seems like you guys parted on good terms. . . .

BETH

Oh, sure. . . .

KRISTY

Well—did you or didn't you?

BETH

Oh, you know. It was pretty amicable. Plus, you know . . . time heals all wounds. . . .

KRISTY

Jesus Christ.

BETH

Kristy. I need you to tell me that this is okay.

KRISTY

To tell you that this is *what?*

BETH

Or, well. To tell me that it's not a total disaster, at least.

KRISTY

Baby, this is a total fucking disaster. . . . God, I was such a bitch to Steven, snapping at him like that when he just got off the plane.

BETH

Well, fine, but don't feel bad, for God's sake.

KRISTY

I wish he hadn't come so early. The wedding isn't even for another week.

BETH

I know.

KRISTY

He's here now, though. We can't leave him languishing in the living room forever.

BETH

I guess now that there's another Texan in the house we'd better revert back to our old Southern hospitality.

KRISTY

I guess. Sure.

BETH

Do you want to, I don't know, hang out with him? Here, I'll go get him. You just rest here. Try to relax.

KRISTY

I'm fine.

BETH

Yeah, right. Whatever.

KRISTY

Okay. . . . Thanks, honey.

BETH

No problem.

Beth leaves the room, crossing back over to the side of the stage where Steven is waiting. The lights come up there as they dim on the side where Kristy continues to sit.

BETH

Hey.

STEVEN

Hey.

BETH

You can come and join us, if you feel like it.

STEVEN

Sure. And, hey, it really is good to see you again, Beth.

BETH

Sure. It's good to see you again, too. It's completely insane. But it's good.

STEVEN

Yeah. We should set aside some time to get caught up.

BETH

Oh, well—you're staying with us, so we'll be hanging out a lot, right?! Plus, you know—all those years and years of being in-laws that lie ahead of us.

STEVEN

No, but I mean—we should set aside some time for just us.

BETH

Yeah. . . .

STEVEN

I mean, I got here early so that I could hang out with you guys and stuff! The wedding isn't even for another week!

BETH

Yeah, we were just saying that. . . .

STEVEN

I know you're super-busy and all! I just mean maybe a couple hours at a bar. Just to get caught up.

BETH

Yeah. . . . You know, I kinda don't want to be alone with you, Steven.

STEVEN

Oh yeah?

BETH

I kind of really don't.

STEVEN

All that was so long ago, I figured we would've both put any bad feelings behind us. . . .

BETH

It isn't that I have any hard feelings, I just. . . . I kind of don't think it would be appropriate for us to hang out alone together.

STEVEN

Okay. *(Pause.)* I mean, do I . . . do I scare you or something? . . .

BETH

Oh, no, no, no! I just, I guess I just feel like there's a really good chance that you'll do something inappropriate.

Pause.

STEVEN

Okay.

BETH

But Kristy wants to see you! Come on, let's go talk to her.

As Beth and Steven "exit" towards Kristy's side of the stage, the lights go down.

Lights up on Kristy sorting laundry. Enter Steven after a moment, having just woken up. He's in boxers and a T-shirt.

STEVEN

Hey.

KRISTY

Hey, good morning.

STEVEN

Where's Beth at?

KRISTY

Work.

STEVEN

God. I feel too woozy for that kind of shit, after last night. She must be tough.

KRISTY

Well, you drank more than anyone else, Steven.

STEVEN

Mm. Story of my life.

Pause. Kristy continues to sort laundry, doesn't really look at Steven.

STEVEN

Remind me of the name of the place we had dinner last night?

KRISTY

The Athenos Diner.

STEVEN

Yeah, that's right. . . . . Those gyros were nice.

KRISTY *

They were.

STEVEN

They sure were. *(Pause.)* Of course, it *was* a Greek diner. . . .

KRISTY

True.

STEVEN

Yeah, I mean if the gyros *weren't* good, then you'd be, like, Whoa. . . .

KRISTY

Exactly.

Pause. There should be a bantering quality to the following exchange. They both know how awkward the situation is and, despite remaining self-conscious, are making fun of it.

STEVEN

So. What's been going on?

KRISTY

You already asked me that.

STEVEN

Did I?

KRISTY

Couple dozen times.

STEVEN

What did you answer?

KRISTY

I think I said "nothing much."

STEVEN

Ah.

Pause. Kristy keeps sorting.

STEVEN

Did I ask how you've been?

KRISTY

I think so.

STEVEN

I don't guess you remember what your answer was? . . .

KRISTY

I think I probably said I was fine? . . .

STEVEN

Ah. Yeah. That rings a bell.

Pause. Kristy keeps sorting her laundry.

STEVEN

I guess I feel like maybe we still haven't broken the ice.

KRISTY

I wonder why that is.

STEVEN

Do you mean you wonder why we haven't broken it, or you wonder why I feel like we haven't broken it?

KRISTY

Don't really care which.

STEVEN

Come on, Kristy, this is dumb.

KRISTY
(keeping control of herself)

You had sex with her.

Pause.

STEVEN

Yeah.

KRISTY

With my wife.

STEVEN

Well. With your fiancée. *(Kristy gives him a look.)* But. I mean. I don't want to split hairs. . . .

KRISTY

That's some pretty thick ice.

STEVEN

Well, then . . . then go at with a *hammer!* You know what I mean? I mean, we're family, right? So stop all this polite bullshit. The whole point of being in a family is that you don't have to pussyfoot around this way! You can really let go on me, you can really let me have it! And then it'll sort of be done, and the air will be cleared.

Pause. Then Kristy finally stops sorting and turns to look at Steven.

KRISTY

Family, huh?

STEVEN

We're family. I'm here for your wedding, aren't I? And so what if there doesn't happen to be a biological connection, we still grew up together. From the time we were ten and twelve years old, anyway.

KRISTY

I'm sorry. That was a bitchy thing to say. Of course, we're family.

STEVEN

I remember meeting you, just before my mom and your dad got married. My mom was like, "You're about to meet Kristy; she's going to be your little sister." That just blew my mind. It was like, all of a sudden, you'd always been my sister; I just hadn't known anything about you until now.

KRISTY

How long had they been dating before that?

STEVEN

Four months or something. They didn't want us to meet until

149

they were sure they were getting married, because they figured it would be such a strain on us if they broke up later. But then they had to hurry up and get married, because it was so awkward to keep you and me from meeting each other.

KRISTY
They got married in too much of a hurry.

STEVEN
Being divorced suits them. I'm glad I got a sister out of it, though.

KRISTY
(softening)
Yeah. Ya big lug.

STEVEN
You know, marriage in general never struck me as a great idea.

KRISTY
Present company excepted, I'm assuming.

STEVEN
You and Beth are great together.

KRISTY
Yeah.

STEVEN
But I just mean . . . I mean, *marriage* . . . I mean, you were always so unconventional. . . .

KRISTY
Yeah, well. If I was unconventional it was only because it happened to work out that way. It wasn't, like, my ambition. There's nothing more pathetic than someone whose whole mission in life is to be "unconventional". . . . Well, maybe in Texas it kind of made sense to be that way. . . .

STEVEN
I just mean, the *idea* of marriage. If two people want to be a

monogamous couple, that's great! But why put a label on it? There's something neurotic about that. If you feel this big need to put your stamp on another person—to brand them with your last name like they were a cow—then maybe you don't trust them as much as you think you do. Not deep down.

KRISTY

First of all, Beth and I are both keeping our own names. . . .

STEVEN

I don't want to start a fight. Just, why should people have to be locked down that way? Why can't things be a little freer? A little more natural?

KRISTY

Because, Steven. Love is a zero-sum game and you have to make a choice. This person *instead of* that one. You can't play loosey-goosey with that stuff or shit gets fucked up fast.

Steven comes up behind Kristy, put his arm around her waist and his face near hers.

STEVEN

Aw, when did my little sis get to be such a hard-ass? . . .

KRISTY
(shaking free)
Hey, we don't do that anymore. . . .

STEVEN

Wha. . . . Of course not! You don't think I—

KRISTY

Just keep your hands to yourself.

STEVEN

Kristy! That wasn't what I meant!

KRISTY

Well good, because that whole Brady Bunch trip is *over.*

STEVEN

I know that. It was a long time ago. . . . We were kids, Kristy. We were thirteen. . . .

KRISTY

I was thirteen. *You* were *fifteen.*

STEVEN

That's right. But still. We were just kids, was all, alone in that house. It wasn't our fault.

KRISTY

I know it wasn't my fault.

STEVEN

We were really young. It was a hormone thing. But it doesn't need to have any effect on the way we are with each other now.

KRISTY

It won't have any effect. But just don't . . . don't remind me of it. When you touch me that way . . . you remind me of it.

Pause.

STEVEN

Well then I won't touch you that way anymore.

Pause.

KRISTY

Listen, I have to finish sorting the laundry.

STEVEN

Can I help you?

KRISTY

No, I can't make you do that. . . . You should go out and be a tourist for a while. . . .

STEVEN

Come on, Kristy. I came to see you.

Pause.

KRISTY

Okay.

Steven begins helping with the laundry. They work silently a while.

KRISTY

What do you want to do this evening?

STEVEN

No idea. What did you guys have in mind?

KRISTY

I don't know. A bar. Then dinner. You want to stick around Queens or head into Manhattan?

STEVEN

It doesn't matter to me.

KRISTY

Oh my God, we're going to be stuck here for hours, both of us insisting that the other one decide. . . .

STEVEN

All right, all right, all right. Let's hang around the neighborhood. Be kind of homey.

KRISTY

Really?! Are you sure you wouldn't rather go into the city?!

STEVEN

Oh my God!

KRISTY

All right, all right. . . .

STEVEN

If you're going to let me decide, let me decide—if you want to go to Manhattan, we'll go to Manhattan! . . .

153

KRISTY

All right! We'll go out in the neighborhood. There's a bar right across from the Off-Track Betting place a couple blocks away. We can start there. You see lots of characters there.

STEVEN

Cool.

Pause. They sort laundry.

STEVEN

You know, Kristy. . . .

KRISTY

Yes?

STEVEN

I wish you weren't scared of me. *(Pause.)* I've never been really quite sure what it was I did. *(Pause.)* I guess part of the reason I came up here was to . . . I don't know . . . get back to the way we used to be. *(Pause.)* Kristy—

KRISTY

I don't want to talk about this.

STEVEN

I just—

KRISTY

Don't want to. *(Pause.)* Thank you for coming to my wedding. I'm grateful. Especially since no one else from the family is, except for Maria and Danny. You're my brother, and I love you. *(Pause.)* Okay?

STEVEN

Sure. Yeah, okay.

KRISTY

All right. So for now . . . let's just leave it at that. . . .

STEVEN

Whatever you say.

They go back to folding laundry.

Scene changes—the lights go down, come up on Steven, Beth, and Kristy at a bar. They have wine glasses, or shot glasses.

STEVEN
So this is your regular bar?

KRISTY
Well. Not our *regular* bar. This is sort of our people-watching bar.

STEVEN
There sure are a lot of broken-down old weirdos wandering around, I'll give it that. And it's because of that place across the street? . . . What *is* OTB, anyway?

KRISTY
Off-Track Betting.

BETH
These old guys go in there and watch the horses run around on these little TVs and they bet on them. Then they come across the street to here and drink.

STEVEN
Horse-racing, huh. So it's like a sport.

KRISTY
Broadly defined, yeah.

BETH
It sort of is to sports what death by tertiary syphilis is to falling in love.

STEVEN
Some of these guys are a little depressing.

KRISTY
Beth likes to make up stories about the more interesting-looking ones.

STEVEN

Oh, yeah? What kind of stories?

BETH

No, nothing. Goofing around, that's all.

STEVEN

Tell one! Make one up about somebody, right now.

BETH

No. It's just a game me and Kristy sometimes play.

Pause.

STEVEN

You know, that's the thing about Beth. She's really observant, and she has a good imagination. She's witty. I've missed that, over the years.

BETH

Yeah. . . .

Pause.

BETH
(cheerfully)

Awkward!

KRISTY

Yup.

STEVEN

Yeah, hey, guys, sorry I'm being so. . . . I'm still just stunned to see Beth here!

BETH

No shit!

KRISTY

Beth and I always talk about how it's funny that we had to come to New York to meet, when she grew up in Fort Worth and I grew up east of Dallas. *(to Steven)* *We* grew up east of Dallas. . . . *(to Beth)* But I guess God thought it would be just too bizarre if *both* of us independently met you there in Texas.

BETH

Sure, go ahead, blame God. Kristy only believes in God when bad things happen. Good things are meaningless chance. Bad things are proof of a willfully malevolent universe. . . . Uh. . . . Not that bumping into you is bad. . . . Shit. . . .

STEVEN

You meant "bad" in the Michael Jackson sense.

BETH

Right.

STEVEN

Sorry your dad is being so pathetic about this whole thing. . . . My *mom* wants to come, actually. But, you know. . . .

KRISTY

Since she's not actually my mother. . . .

STEVEN

Right, and since she and your dad aren't even speaking anymore. . . . But so the cousins are coming, though.

KRISTY

Yeah. I was going to call them later.

Pause.

STEVEN

So. How did. . . .

Steven gestures at Beth and Kristy.

BETH

How did we meet?

STEVEN

Sure.

BETH

Well . . . nothing fancy. . . .

KRISTY

We were both volunteering one night a week at this bookstore
in Soho. Housing Works. It's this charity—the books are all
donated, most of the staff are volunteers, and the proceeds go to
homeless people with AIDS.

STEVEN

That's nice.

KRISTY

Yeah, well. You work there four hours a week, and it's all
pretty laid-back. That's where we're having the wedding. We're
renting it, they're closing it for during our wedding. It's a really
neat space, and there's a big open area where we can fit all our
friends.

STEVEN

I was wondering about that. Did it ever occur to you that maybe
the reason your redneck families don't think it's a real wedding
is because it's in a bookstore? And not because you're gay?

KRISTY

Ha ha.

BETH

Anyway, Kristy and I both worked the Wednesday night shift.
We shelved books together. Dorkiest courtship ever. Then one
night they closed the store and held a party for the volunteers,
with lots of booze. And Kristy and I wound up making out in
a corner, behind the used-LP displays.

KRISTY

I hadn't even been sure she was gay.

STEVEN

I can see how that might be confusing.

KRISTY

Well. So how about you two?

BETH

You mean, how did we meet?

KRISTY

Question of the hour, right?

STEVEN

You sure you want to, uh, hear about it? . . .

BETH

Yeah, it might be a little awkward. . . .

KRISTY

Oh, I'm sure it will be awkward, but I'm already drunk, so we may as well go for it now.

BETH

Well. I was in this bar. This really crowded bar, and this guy had just bought me a drink, but I'd decided I didn't want to talk to him anymore and so I had turned to face the other way. And Steven approached me from that direction.

KRISTY

Taking advantage of the other guy's weakness.

STEVEN

Kicking others while they're down. Secret of success, in love.

BETH

Anyway, he walked up to me and he held out his sleeve, and he said, "Here, feel this material." And I did, I reached out and kind of rubbed his arm, because I was a little drunk, and because actually the shirt really did seem like nice material. And Steven said, "You feel that? That's boyfriend material."

KRISTY

He said that?

STEVEN

Sure.

KRISTY

Wow. That's hilarious.

STEVEN

Thank you.

KRISTY

Who knew my big brother was such a stud muffin?

STEVEN

When inspiration struck. Although that's the only time I ever did that.

BETH

What? You mean that's the only time you ever used the "boyfriend material" line? Even though it worked?

STEVEN

No, that's not what I mean. . . .

BETH

Good, because that one's priceless. . . .

STEVEN

I just meant that was the only time I ever approached a woman in a bar.

Pause.

BETH

What?

STEVEN

That was the only time I ever approached anyone that way. Still is the only time. I saw you there and I thought: This is it. If I don't go talk to that woman, I'll always regret it.

Pause.

BETH

Yeah, it's funny how this stuff can work out! . . .

KRISTY

And so then you guys were a couple, right? It wasn't just a casual thing?

BETH

Well. . . .

STEVEN

We were a couple.

BETH

We were . . . you know. I mean it wasn't a one-night *stand*. . . .
I mean we saw each other. . . .

STEVEN

We were a couple! We're not a couple now. Obviously. But we
were a couple then.

BETH

We went out on dates. But I don't know if we were "dating."
Like, exclusively.

STEVEN

I thought we were. I wasn't seeing anyone else. Were you seeing
anyone else?

KRISTY

Yeah, how many people were you seeing, Beth?

BETH

I guess that, no, I wasn't seeing anyone else. But I *could* have
seen other people and it wouldn't have felt like cheating.

STEVEN

Well. I guess it would have felt that way to me.

KRISTY

And you guys went out for more than two months, right?

STEVEN

Seven and a half weeks.

BETH

There were whole weeks in there where we didn't actually see
each other.

STEVEN

Well. We saw each other every weekend, at least. We both had work and our apartments weren't really close by.

BETH

I don't think we did see each other every weekend, actually.

STEVEN

I know we did.

BETH

Well, it's been years. One of us might be misremembering.

STEVEN

No . . . I remember it all pretty well. . . .

KRISTY

You know, *we've* gone a week without seeing each other before. And *we're* a pretty serious couple.

BETH

We went a week apart because you had to go out of town. Anyway, what does that have to do with anything?

Pause.

STEVEN

Is that your phone vibrating?

KRISTY

Oh, you're right. . . . *(She digs her phone out of her purse.)* It's Maria! *(She answers it.)* Hey, Maria! How're you doing? *(Kristy's smile fades.)* What do you mean? *(Pause.)* Well. The wedding is . . . I mean, we were expecting you guys to drive in Thursday . . . so I. . . . *(Pause.)* Hang on, hang on. *(Kristy stands up, flustered.)* I'm, uh, I'm going to walk around the block while I take this. . . .

BETH

What is it, honey?

KRISTY

What do you think? ... Here. ... *(Kristy clumsily digs through her bag.)* I think I owe, uh. ...

BETH

Don't worry about it, honey. ...

KRISTY

I can pay. ...

BETH

For God's sake, don't *worry* about it. ...

KRISTY

Here! (Kristy throws some money on the table.) I'll meet you guys back at the apartment later on. ...

Exit Kristy.

BETH

Shit.

STEVEN

Doesn't sound like those cousins are coming.

BETH

God.

Beth gathers the money, the check, puts it together.

STEVEN

Here, what do I owe. ...

BETH

No, nothing, we said we were going to treat you. ... God, this is humiliating.

STEVEN

Our families suck.

BETH

Our families suck donkey.

STEVEN

Should we just head back, or . . . maybe get another drink, or go grab another one someplace else. . . .

BETH

Oh, no, I want to be there when she gets back. . . .

STEVEN

Sure, sure. . . . *(Pause. They get up from the table, or bar.)* I am glad to be alone with you for a few minutes, anyway. I mean, too bad about the circumstances. . . .

Beth smiles tightly, doesn't answer. Beth and Steven walk away from the table. The scene shifts. They move to the other side of the room, as the lights change and indicate the passage of time and distance.

STEVEN

Here we are, home sweet home. . . .

BETH

Oh, this apartment is such a wreck, I'm so embarrassed. . . .

STEVEN

Hey, don't worry, we're family now.

BETH

That's true. . . .

STEVEN

It's not completely a disaster, is it?

BETH

What isn't?

STEVEN

Us being a family now. I mean, you did *like* me. And it's not like I ever did anything really bad to you.

BETH

No, you never did. I just could feel that it wasn't going to work out.

STEVEN

Well, maybe in a way it did work out. Like, we're not a couple, but we get the chance to know each other. It didn't work out romantically, but we still get to have this relationship that isn't going to go away.

BETH

Sure.

STEVEN

So what if we don't have any of the physical stuff? What I missed the most was the friend stuff. And now we get to have that, and we don't have to worry about about any of that romance getting in the way, because, obviously, if you're married to my sister, then. . . .

BETH

Sure. Obviously. . . . You could be a fun guy sometimes. And you did have a kind of . . . intensity, I guess. Sometimes.

STEVEN

I always had fun with you, too. Occasionally I did maybe get carried away.

BETH

No, don't worry about any of that old stuff. I'm glad that . . . well . . . I'm glad.

STEVEN

Me, too.

BETH

Well. . . . Hey, you wanna help me with these favors for the wedding reception?

STEVEN

What?

BETH

Kristy has this tragically labor-intensive idea for the party favors. We're having sushi catered, and for the party favors we're passing out these halfway-nice pairs of chopsticks that have our names printed on them. Like, one chopstick has "Beth" printed on it. And the other one has "Kristy" printed on it. And they're joined together with these pink ribbons.

STEVEN
Wow.

BETH
It's symbolic. Get it?

STEVEN
You guys are serving sushi at the reception? With chopsticks?

BETH
Yup.

STEVEN
Well no wonder no one from our family's coming. . . .

BETH
All right, all right. . . .

STEVEN
You know we're all Texans, don't you? You're a Texan too. . . .

BETH
All right! We got a good deal on the sushi! . . . Anyway. Maybe it would be a nice thing if we could have these all done by the time Kristy gets back. Cheer her up. But for that to happen, human beings are going to have to tie all these chopsticks together with these pink ribbons. So . . . if you could pitch in, that'd be awesome. *(Beth is on the floor. She starts tying the favors together; Steven stands overhead and just watches; after a bit Beth turns to look curiously up at him.)* Or not. It's a free country.

STEVEN
I don't really want to help you put favors together for your wedding reception, Beth.

BETH
Well—that's cool. It *is* a pretty annoying job. . . .

STEVEN

No, that's not what I. . . . The truth is, Beth, I. . . . I was going to be good, I wasn't going to say anything, but—

BETH

Whoa, whoa, whoa—maybe you should follow that instinct. . . .

STEVEN

I think about you, Beth. A lot. And I don't mean just these last couple days. I mean for years I've been thinking about you. About your laugh, and the way your nose crinkles up, and how good it feels to make love to you.

BETH

Okay. You know, that would have been kind of an endearing thing to say to me during the eight weeks that we were dating. Or, sorry, seven and a half. But now that I'm going to be your sister-in-law, I'm not sure it's appropriate.

STEVEN

I started reading up on sexuality after Kristy, you know, came out or whatever you call it. Apparently sexuality is very fluid, according to some people. That's the word some people use, is "fluid."

BETH

Hmmmm.

STEVEN

Which is just an interesting idea because, you know, you'd think that if it can flow one way, then it could also . . . you know . . . flow back.

BETH

Why, yes, I suppose that theoretically that's true.

STEVEN

Not that I care one way or the other about *any* of this stuff. I mean, if gay people want to get married or join the army, well . . . fuck it, I mean, I used to not be able to imagine why anyone would ever want to do either thing, but, hey, no skin off my butt. As for the army, all those words they use to describe that shit—honor, country, patriotism, whatever—I mean, none of those words *mean* anything. And it's kind of the same way with marriage. Almost everyone I ever met who got married wound up getting a divorce. So when people say things like, It's a sacred institution that we need to protect, I used to just think, What are they *talking* about? It's one step up from going steady—it's going really really steady. Who would bother fighting for *that?* On *either* side? . . . But I thought that way before I met you. Because with you . . . even from the first second I saw you, there was this huge, powerful connection. Even before we spoke. Something so primal, so basic. . . .

BETH

Steven. Look. These kinds of declarations, they work sometimes in movies or in books or in plays. But in real life, they're a little embarrassing. Not to mention, once again, that I'm a lesbian. Not to mention that Kristy will be coming back any second, and she's already upset, and she's your sister, and I'm going to marry her. . . .

STEVEN

What're you afraid of?

BETH

Nothing!

STEVEN

Afraid to hear me out? Afraid I'll bring you around?

BETH

Okay, you know what? Go ahead. Get it out of your system. Get it *all* out. Because I swear to God we are never going to have a conversation like this ever again.

STEVEN

Don't you hear what I'm telling you? For me to ask you what I asked you, feeling the way I did about that stuff. . . . Do you know what your reaction did to me?

BETH

You asked me to marry you because I told you I might be a lesbian.

STEVEN

That wasn't *why!* . . .

BETH

I said to you, Hey, listen, Steven, I think I might actually be more into women than men. And your reaction was to be, like, Marry me! . . . And you know, I've been wondering . . . why was it such a shock when I opened that door? Why did it never occur to you, when Kristy told you she was going to marry a woman from Fort Worth named Beth, why didn't it occur to you that maybe, just maybe, it was the same Beth from Fort Worth that you once proposed to? Who told you she thought she was a lesbian?

STEVEN

Of course it never occurred to me! What were the odds?

BETH

But that it would never even occur to you? . . . Here's what I think. I think you're telling the truth. I don't think it did occur to you. I think you didn't even pay attention to my name or anything else when Kristy told you about me.

STEVEN

I knew she was marrying someone named *Beth!*

BETH

But I don't think you *paid attention.* I don't think you cared what my name was or where I was from. So why are you here at all? I bet you came up here to fuck up Kristy's wedding.

STEVEN

What?!

BETH

I think you got up here and you saw me and you switched your attention my way. But I bet that even if it hadn't been me . . . I think you're the type who wants to hold on to people. Like you own them. You don't want Kristy to have me. But you wouldn't have wanted anyone else to have Kristy, either.

STEVEN
Beth, this is crazy talk. What have I done to make you think that?

BETH
I don't know. I just have a feeling. I see how you would feel like you had some claim on *me*, because we slept together. That's why you asked me to marry you, all those years ago. Was that you couldn't stand to let go of this claim you'd staked. I'm not sure yet why you would feel that way about Kristy. But I do know that Kristy's always felt weird about you.

STEVEN
You want to know why I asked you to marry me? Because you're my soulmate. And that means I'm *your* soulmate, so you can't afford not to listen to me. There was something between us. Whatever that connection was—chemical, whatever—it was so powerful that it may as well have been magic. I just mean that I know, *without question,* that we are supposed to be together. You're the only person I've ever felt that way with.

BETH
We kind of didn't have all that much in common, Steven.

STEVEN
Superficially, maybe not. But in our souls . . . in our hearts . . . in our whatevers . . . if we'd lived in a different time . . . in a different society . . . someplace with less distractions . . . someplace more natural . . . you would never have left me. But here—in America, in the twenty-first century—there's all these bells and whistles. Everybody's thinking about what city to move to next, everybody's shopping for their next lifestyle. But if we could just . . . if we could just have met in a little place, where we knew all the rules, and where there weren't a million strangers popping in and out all the time. . . .

170

BETH

I am so losing patience with you, Steven. . . .

STEVEN

Beth, I'm talking about our lives here! We have a chance to
make our lives mean something! You know how long I've been
thinking about you?! You don't have the right to throw away
what we had on a *whim!*

BETH

How mean do I have to be to you, Steven?! Okay, you know
what? You were *cute.* You were *cute.* That was *it.* When you
came up to me that first time, I thought, "There's not a lot to this
guy, but he's kind of minimally appealing, and I have nothing,
nothing else going on, so why not?" You know why I went with
you? Because it was just such a fucking aimless, lost period in
my life! And because at first it never even occurred to me that
you were interested in anything other than getting laid, because
as far as I could tell there wasn't much of anything to you! You
were just sort of this silly cute pretentious goofball! And then
when you started getting creepy and obsessive I didn't see any
point in putting up with it, because there just wasn't enough *to*
you to make it worth my while!

STEVEN

Cute, huh? That's what you think of me? Is that I'm cute, huh?

BETH

Not so much, anymore! Not right at the moment! Right now
you strike me as a selfish asshole with mental problems!

STEVEN

You fucking dyke.

*Steven lunges for Beth, grabs her, almost seems to be trying to choke
her but is in fact trying to kiss her; Beth pushes his face away,
struggles to break free.*

BETH

Let go of me! *(Beth fights him; she punches him in the ear*

171

repeatedly; Steven releases her, collapses to his knees, covers his face.)
I could *kill* you! Fucking *kill* you! *(Beth walks around, trying to blow off steam. Returns to stand over Steven.)* I don't want to see you anymore. And I mean, at all. I think you're crazy, I think you're dangerous. As for *disrespectful*, I just . . . I . . . I mean, the time to use *that* word was like ten *minutes* ago! . . . I don't care if you're Kristy's brother, or *step*-brother, or *whatever the fuck you are*, I don't want to ever see you again, and I don't want her to see you, either! You are not her brother anymore! Do you get me?! *(Long pause. Steven is weeping with rage, trying to stifle the noise. Beth keeps walking it off, then sits.)* Stop crying. *(Pause.)* Steven? Stop crying, okay? Kristy's going to be back any second.

Steven kind of pulls it together. They sit in silence. Pretty long pause. Enter Kristy—she's also been crying. Steven is still visibly upset—his eyes are still red, maybe his cheeks are still wet, etc.

KRISTY
What happened?
Beth and Steven look at each other. Beth casts around for an explanation, then gives up.

BETH
We had a fight.

KRISTY
Oh.

BETH
How are you?

KRISTY
Nobody's coming. Not from my family. Except for Steven.

BETH
Oh, honey.

KRISTY
It's okay. I kind of expected that. Right? I said this would happen.

BETH

Yeah.

KRISTY

Still. I guess I thought maybe. . . . I mean, you'd think that, what with all the combinations of parents I've had, at least one of them. . . . Well, fuck it. You know, I'm glad. That you won't be subjected to their crap. It's not worth the pain. They want to ostracize us? Fine, let them stay away. They're doing us a favor.

STEVEN

They'll come around.

KRISTY

Fuck 'em. I don't care if they do or not. What does it matter if they don't want to meet Beth? It's their loss, not Beth's.

STEVEN

It's Beth's, too. That's the whole point of getting married, right? Is that you have to put up with all the other person's crap.

BETH

I don't know if that's the *point* of it, Steven.

STEVEN

Well, isn't it? I always thought that was the point. Was that you had to deal with all the other person's garbage and history. I thought that was what made it more like real life, instead of just playing around, the way dating is. You can't just go back to your own apartment if you get pissed off at the other person. And you share debts. If they get sick, then you have to go bankrupt along with them. And that nutty old bitch, she isn't just your girlfriend's mom anymore, she's your mother-in-law. All those shitty, stupid relatives of your girlfriend—they're not none of your business anymore. You're stuck with them, just as much as she is.

BETH
(sarcastically, looking hard at Steven)

Oh . . . boy.

STEVEN
I'm not saying any of that's a good thing, necessarily. All I'm saying is that that's what marriage *is*. As far as I could ever tell.

KRISTY
Well! That's cheerful! So what do you say, Beth? You still want me? Shitty family, deep emotional scarring, and all? *(Beth looks at Kristy and starts to cry.)* Honey?! What is it?

BETH
Yes. I do.

Kristy takes Beth into her arms. Steven stands up.

STEVEN
I'm going to, uh, just step into the other room. . . .

Kristy nods. Exit Steven.

KRISTY
What is it, honey?

BETH
I don't know. Brides are supposed to cry, right?

KRISTY
Our wedding isn't for about a week.

BETH
I'm so excited I wanted to get a head start.

KRISTY
Don't try to distract me by being mushy, tell me what's wrong.

BETH
Nothing, nothing. Or, I don't know. I haven't eaten all day.

KRISTY
Didn't you have breakfast?

BETH
I had an apple at one.

KRISTY

Jesus, honey! It's almost eight o'clock.

BETH

I was going to eat. But then I forgot.

KRISTY

Well, we had better get some food in you.

BETH

Okay. *(Pause.)* Can we have Mexican?

KRISTY

If you promise that you'll still be able to fit in your dress.

BETH

No promises.

KRISTY

Are you sure that's all it is?

BETH

Yeah.

KRISTY

You're sure it doesn't have anything to do with that fight you and Steven had?

Beth sits up, pulling herself together; she takes her compact out of her purse, wipes her face, powders it, is all business.

BETH

Oh, no. I just suddenly felt light-headed. Plus I'm jittery about the wedding and all, and plus I guess it did kind of get to me, your family being such assholes.

KRISTY

The thing is . . . what was the fight about, Beth?

BETH

We were kind of talking and I guess it kind of came out that he still has kind of a thing for me.

175

KRISTY

That kind of sounds like kind of a big deal.

BETH

Not really. I mean, it was emotional. He can't help it, I guess. I put him in his place. It wasn't super-pleasant but, you know. . . .

KRISTY

Well . . . he can't be disrespectful. . . .

BETH

He had a moment of weakness. Let's just take the high road about it. It's not exactly a relaxing situation, for any of us.

KRISTY

Yeah. Sorry, I shouldn't have unloaded on you earlier.

BETH

Yes you should have.

KRISTY

Well . . . should we take him to dinner with us?

BETH

Of course.

KRISTY

Are you sure? He can fend for himself for one meal. If you're upset right now. . . . I mean, obviously it makes you tense that you have this crazy past with my brother. . . .

BETH

I have a future with him, too. As my brother-in-law. So it doesn't make sense to start ignoring him now.

KRISTY

If you're sure. . . .

BETH

Kristy. He came all this way to see you. To see *you*. And to be a part of our wedding.

KRISTY

Why do I get the feeling that this is part of the "worse" in the "for better or for worse" bit?

BETH

Honey. This is all very complicated. Let's not drive ourselves crazy trying to understand every little piece of it. Let's just hang on and go through with it.

Pause.

KRISTY

Okay. *(They join hands, are about to exit to go meet Steven. Then Kristy hesitates.)* Although, you know. I *do* wish he hadn't gotten to town so early. Things were already stressful enough, just with the wedding plans.

BETH

Well. He's family.

KRISTY

Yeah, closest thing to it, anyway.

BETH

Well. . . . I mean, all I want is to do the right thing.

KRISTY

I know that, babe.

BETH

And this is it. Right?

KRISTY

Sure it is. He's upset. We're upset, but so is he. So we should be nice to him.

BETH

Yeah, and . . . that stuff he said . . . it's true, right? You can't just pick and choose, when it comes to family. You have to take the good with the bad.

KRISTY

Right.

Pause.

BETH

Except. . . .

KRISTY

Honey? What is it?

Pause.

BETH

Do you know that he called me a fucking dyke and then, like, attacked me so that I had to punch him in the ear to get him off me?

KRISTY

What?!

BETH

And he also asked me to marry him.

KRISTY

In . . . in that order? . . .

BETH

No . . . no, the chronology is sort of. . . . There's stuff about me and Steven that I guess I never told you. That I guess I should have.

KRISTY

Well. Same here.

BETH

Well. . . . Let's go get him, I guess. Where should we have dinner? . . .

KRISTY

What?! Are you in shock?! If he attacked you or if he even just upset you then I am gonna kick him right the fuck outta here!

BETH

Well . . . you know . . . he was upset . . . and we do have this pretty intense past . . . I guess I wasn't really honest with you about just how intense it was. . . .

KRISTY

Fuck all that! This is New York City! We moved away from home, we don't have to be *nice,* and we can do what we want! I'm gonna marry you and our families and the government can all go to hell, and we're not going to have anyone in our apartment that we don't want there! . . . Wait a second. . . . Is my brother that freak you told me about? Who proposed to you when you told him you might be gay? . . .

BETH

Uh . . . if I'd known it was your brother I was telling you about I wouldn't have called him a *freak.* . . .

KRISTY

Oh, *hell* no. . . .

BETH

Kristy, hold on, I . . . I love you. You're going to be my wife. No matter what the law says—*I* say you will be. And if you. . . . I know that your family is important to you. I know it hurts you, how distant you are from them. I know how much you want to reconnect with them. And so . . . don't feel like you have to do anything for my sake. Not anything. I don't *want* you to burn any bridges. I know you want your family here, and I know how important it is to you, so I don't mind putting up with . . . with anything. Kristy, I would put up with anything for you.

Pause. Then Kristy gives Beth a big kiss on the mouth—not necessarily a sexy kiss, with tongue and open mouths—her palms pressed up against Beth's cheeks.

KRISTY

Sweetcheeks, I am gonna burn. That. Bridge.

STEVEN
(calling from off-stage)
Hey! You girls wanna maybe watch TV for a while or something?

KRISTY
It won't really even be that huge of a sacrifice.

BETH
I guess there are bigger things I could ask you for.

KRISTY
Think about what they are and then ask me for them. I want
you to ask me.

STEVEN
(off-stage)
You guys? . . .

KRISTY
Let's do it.

BETH
Okay.

KRISTY
(singing out, as she and Beth exit, arm-in-arm)
Oh, *Steeee-ven!* . . .

BLACKOUT

PRODUCTION
NOTES

THE VICTIM

The Victim was first performed as part of the 2010 Midtown International Theatre Festival's Short Subjects. It was paired with *School Romance,* and presented under the title *Reunion Plays.* Performances were on July 19th, July 20th, and July 23rd.

April – Tiffany Esteb
Grace – Jessica Vera
Directed by Kelly Kay Griffith.

In November 2010 *The Victim* was performed as part of *The Victim (and Other Short Plays),* again starring Tiffany Esteb and Jessica Vera, again directed by Kelly Kay Griffith. Performance dates were November 11th, 12th, 17th, 18th, 19th, and 20th. The other plays presented were *The Tracks Are Electrified,* by Jane Miller, directed by Brandi Varnell; *The Airport,* written and directed by Alec Gutherz; and *Memory,* by Pamela Scott, directed by Barrett Hileman.

The Victim was given a reading at the Society for Ethical Culture on January 19th, 2011.

April – Tiffany Esteb
Grace – Kelly Kay Griffith
Directed by Kathryn McConnell.

When *The Victim* was produced, I realized that in the time it had taken me to write it, the play had already become a period piece—Grace wants to order food but can't because April's phone has been shut off. Today one inevitably wonders why Grace doesn't use her cell phone. But when the scene was written, there were no smart phones and people didn't automatically carry cells around with them.

SCHOOL ROMANCE

School Romance was first performed as part of the 2010 Midtown International Theatre Festival's Short Subjects. It was paired with *The Victim,* both of which were presented under the title *Reunion Plays.* Performances were on July 19th, July 20th, and July 23rd.

Wendy – Lori Lane Jefferson
Leslie – Cavan Hallman
Directed by Dina Epshteyn.

School Romance was next produced as part of Sticky, on March 18th, 2011.

Wendy – Marisa Viola
Leslie – James Daniel
Directed by Jeannine Jones.

PORNOPHILES

Pornophiles was performed as part of the Shortened Attention Span Festival, on June 4th, 5th, 6th, and 7th, 2009.

Preston – Jeffrey Kitrosser
Miranda – Megan Buzzard
Directed by Kenneth Ruth.

Pornophiles was performed as part of the John Chatterton's Short Plays Lab on December 19th and 20th, 2009.

Preston – Ronan Babbit
Miranda – Emily Kunkel
Directed by Morgan Gould.

SIBLING RIBALDRY

Sibling Ribaldry was first produced as part of the Shortened Attention Span Festival, on October 15th, 16th, 17th, and 18th, 2009.

Penny – Elizabeth Lee
Frankie – Farrah Crane
Toby – Daniel Holmes
Directed by Kenneth Ruth.

Sibling Ribaldry was produced a second time as part of the John Chatterton's Short Plays Lab, on February 6th and 7th, 2010.

Penny – Farrah Crane
Frankie – Evelyn Sullivan
Toby – Jason Ellis
Directed by Kenneth Ruth.

A BEAUTIFUL CIRCLE OF LOVE AND ACCEPTANCE

A Beautiful Circle of Love and Acceptance was produced as part of the Shortened Attention Span Festival, on June 10th, 11th, 12th, and 13th, 2010.
Graham – Marcus Conerly
Phil – William Kozy
Tracy – Kelly Kay Griffith
Directed by Kathryn McConnell.

LOVE STINKS

Love Stinks was produced as part of the Shortened Attention Span Festival, on October 7th, 8th, 9th, and 10th, 2010.
Brian – Gus Ferrari
Maggie – Jessica Vera
Fiona – Kelly Kay Griffith
Directed by Kathryn McConnell.

The four plays in Part II were going to be produced by Kathryn McConnell and Brandi Varnell as an evening of one-acts called *Sex and Violence (Gratuity Included).* (The plan was that I would write a fifth one-act to fill out the show.) Unfortunately the project didn't happen, for various reasons.

I had originally planned to use *Sex and Violence* as a title heading for Part II. But considering the subject matter of the first piece in this collection, I realized that would be in dubious taste, at best.

SO MEONE BORROWED, SOMEONE SCREWED

Someone Borrowed, Someone Screwed was produced by Squeaky Bicycle, as half of *For Better or Worse.* It was performed in repertory with *Saturday Pleasures,* by Michael Burgan.

Performance dates: July 16th, 17th, and 18th, 2010.
Beth – Brandi Varnell
Steven – Jeff Johnson
Kristy – Melissa Jalali
Directed by Kathryn McConnell.

Kathryn McConnell and Brandi Varnell were kind enough to commission from me a forty-minute play to be performed alongside Michael Burgan's one-act. The only constraint was that both plays should use the same actors *(Saturday Pleasures* was already cast). Since *Saturday Pleasures* was a play about a wedding, I decided that mine would also be about a wedding, so as to provide continuity. To avoid making the evening repetitious, and because two of the actors were actresses, I decided to make mine a lesbian wedding.

This play too is already a period piece. When I wrote the play I didn't know I'd be attending my first legally recognized gay wedding about two years later.

After a performance of *A Beautiful Circle of Love and Acceptance,* a bunch of us went out to a bar. My deadline for getting a script to Kate and Brandi was coming up, and I didn't have anything other than the lesbian-wedding idea, and a sense that the story should be about a triangle (since there were three actors). Kate and Brandi were asking me to at least give them a title so they could start promoting the evening. Margot Machado had come to see *Beautiful Circle,* and we were sitting at the bar together; I asked her what a good title would be for a play about a wedding in which a third party shows up and makes some sort of trouble between the imminent brides. As if the answer to that question were common knowledge, Margot immediately said, "Someone Borrowed, Someone Screwed." I suppose the title doesn't exactly make sense, but I've never been able to think of anything that I liked enough to use instead.

ABOUT THE AUTHOR:

J. Boyett is a playwright, novelist, filmmaker, and founder of Saltimbanque Books. Please visit www.saltimbanquebooks.com or jboyett.net, and sign up for the mailing list.

If you enjoyed this book, please help support it by rating it on Amazon, Goodreads, and any other online forum.

And we hope you'll go to saltimbanquebooks.com and sign up for our mailing list.

Thanks!

ALSO FROM SALTIMBANQUE BOOKS:

BENJAMIN GOLDEN DEVILHORNS,
by Doug Shields

A collection of stories set in a bizarre, almost believable universe: the lord of cockroaches breathes the same air as a genius teenage girl with a thing for criminals, a ruthless meat tycoon who hasn't figured out that secret gay affairs are best conducted out of town, and a telepathic bowling ball. Yes, the bowling ball breathes.

RICKY, by J. Boyett

Ricky's hoping to begin a new life upon his release from prison; but on his second day out, someone murders his sister. Determined to find her killer, but with no idea how to go about it, Ricky follows a dangerous path, led by clues that may only be in his mind.

BROTHEL, by J. Boyett

What to do for kicks if you live in a sleepy college town, and all you need to pass your courses is basic literacy? Well, you could keep up with all the popular TV shows. Or see how much alcohol you can drink without dying. Or spice things up with the occasional hump behind the bushes. And if that's not enough you could start a business....

COMING IN SUMMER 2015:

COLD PLATE SPECIAL, by Rob Widdicombe

Jarvis Henders has finally hit the beige bottom of his beige life, his law-school dreams in shambles, and every bar singing to him to end his latest streak of sobriety. Instead of falling back off the wagon, he decides to go take his life back from the child molester who stole it. But his journey through the looking glass turns into an adventure where he's too busy trying to guess what will come at him next, to dwell on the ghosts of his past.

STEWART AND JEAN, by J. Boyett

A blind date between Stewart and Jean explodes into a confrontation from the past when Jean realizes that theirs is not a random meeting at all, but that Stewart is the brother of the man who once tried to rape her. Or is she the woman who murdered his brother? And will anyone ever know?

THE LITTLE MERMAID: A HORROR STORY, by J. Boyett

Brenna has an idyllic life with her heroic, dashing, lifeguard boyfriend Mark. She knows it's only natural that other girls should have crushes on the guy. But there's something different about the young girl he's rescued, who seemed to appear in the sea out of nowhere—a young girl with strange powers, and who will stop at nothing to have Mark for herself.

I'M YOUR MAN, by F. Sykes

It's New York in the 1990's, and every week for years Fred has cruised Port Authority for hustlers, living a double life, dreaming of the one perfect boy that he can really love. When he meets Adam, he wonders if he's found that perfect boy after all … and even though Adam proves to be very imperfect, and very real, Fred's dream is strengthened to the point that he finds it difficult to awake.

THE UNKILLABLES, by J. Boyett

Gash-Eye already thought life was hard, as the Neanderthal slave to a band of Cro-Magnons. Then zombies attacked, wiping out nearly everyone she knows and separating her from the Jaw, her half-breed son. Now she fights to keep the last remnants of her former captors alive. Meanwhile, the Jaw and his father try to survive as they maneuver the zombie-infested landscape alongside time-travelers from thirty thousand years in the future.... Destined to become a classic in the literature of Zombies vs. Cavemen.

64796457R00115

Made in the USA
Charleston, SC
07 December 2016